A Treatise On the Culture of the Vine and the Art of Making Wine

To

Mr Robt Archie

with the best regards

of the Author

A

TREATISE

ON THE

CULTURE OF THE VINE,

AND THE

ART OF MAKING WINE;

COMPILED FROM THE

WORKS OF CHAPTAL, AND OTHER FRENCH WRITERS;

AND FROM THE

NOTES OF THE COMPILER, DURING A RESIDENCE IN
SOME OF THE WINE PROVINCES OF FRANCE.

BY JAMES BUSBY.

Tot vina, quot agri.——PLINY.

AUSTRALIA:

PRINTED BY R. HOWE, GOVERNMENT PRINTER.

1825.

AUSTRALIA: PRINTED BY R. HOWE.

TO HIS EXCELLENCY

MAJOR GENERAL SIR THOMAS BRISBANE,

K.C.B. L.L.D. F.R.S.L. & E. &c.

GOVERNOR AND COMMANDER IN CHIEF,

IN AND OVER THE TERRITORY OF NEW SOUTH WALES,

AND ITS DEPENDENCIES.

THE FOLLOWING TREATISE,

BEING AN HUMBLE ATTEMPT

TO PROMOTE THE ADVANCEMENT OF

THE INTERESTING COLONIES UNDER HIS COMMAND,

IS MOST RESPECTFULLY INSCRIBED,

BY HIS OBEDIENT HUMBLE SERVANT,

THE AUTHOR.

CONTENTS.

INTRODUCTION.

PART I.---CHAP. I.

	Page.
OF THE INFLUENCE OF CLIMATE, SOIL, EXPOSURE, SEASONS, AND CULTURE, ON THE VINE	1
Climate	2
Soil	7
Exposure	12
Seasons	19
Culture	23

CHAP. II.

OF VARIETIES OF VINES, AND THEIR PROPAGATION BY SEED	29
Varieties from change of Soil, Climate, &c.	36
Varieties from Seed	42
Mixture of Varieties, &c.	46
Description of Varieties	62

CHAP. III.

OF THE PREPARATION OF THE SOIL, THE CHOICE OF PLANTS, AND THE DIFFERENT METHODS OF PLANTING	78
Choice of Plants	80
Season for Planting	83
Methods of Planting	85

CHAP. IV.

OF THE HEIGHT OF VINES, THEIR PRUNING, AND SUPPORTS	88
Height of the Stocks	ibid.
Pruning	90
Props	97
Pinching, unleaving, &c.	99

CHAP. V.

OF LABOURING AND MANURING THE SOIL FOR VINES	102
Labouring of the Soil	ibid.
Instruments of Labour---Manure	105
Taste of the Soil	106

CHAP. VI.

OF THE DISEASES AND ACCIDENTS INCIDENT TO VINES, WITH THE MEANS OF PREVENTION, REMEDY, AND RENEWAL	108
Injuries from Frost	ibid.
Failure of Fructification	110
Diseases from other Causes	111
Disease from Insects	113
Renewal of Plants by Layers	116
Old Age of Vines	119
Preserving Grapes	120
Raisins	122

CONTENTS.

PART II.—CHAP. I.

Of the most favourable period for the vintage, and the method of procedure - 124

CHAP. II.

Of the means of disposing the juice of the grape to fermentation - 131

CHAP. III.

Of the phenomena of fermentation, and the means of managing it - 144
Causes which influence Fermentation - 146
Temperature - ibid.
Atmospheric Air - 150
Volume of the Liquid - 155
Constituent Principles of the Must - 156
Products of Fermentation - 167
Heat - 169
Carbonic Acid - 170
Alcohol - 175
Colour - 178
Management of Fermentation - 180

CHAP. IV.

Of the time and manner of discharging the vat - 184

CHAP. V.

Of the management of wines in the cask - 193
Sulphuring - 198
Racking off - 201
Clarifying - 204
Mixing of Wines - 207
Flavouring of Wines - 211
Vessels proper for containing Wines - 214

CHAP. VI.

Of the degenerations and spontaneous alterations of wines - 219
Ropiness - 223
Ascescence - 228

CHAP. VII.

Of the virtues of wine - 236

CHAP. VIII.

Of the principles contained in wine - 241
Malic Acid - ibid.
Tartar - 244
Aroma - 246
Colouring Principle - ibid.

CHAP. IX.

Of the manufacture of vinegar from wine - 250

CHAP. X.

Of the distillation of wines, - 255

INTRODUCTION.

IN the view of emigrating to New South Wales, the compiler of the following work was led into an examination of the circumstances of that colony, in the course of which, he was particularly struck with the relation in which it stands to the mother country.

Destitute of, or producing in a very inconsiderable degree, any article of produce which might minister to the wants or comforts of Great Britain, and, consequently, incapable of maintaining with her that regular and natural intercourse between a colony and its parent state, which consists in the exchange of the raw produce of the one, for the manufactured commodities of the other, New South Wales seems, till very lately, to have been chiefly dependent on the expenditure of the money of Great Britain, in the subsistence of felons transported to its shores, and in the pay of the establishments necessary for their management and controul; and has, consequently, been considered rather as a necessary and expensive appendage to the judicial institutions of the country, than a colony to which she might look for an extension of her power, or an increase of her trade and resources.

Of late, however, the spirit of emigration has led thither many individuals and families, of a different description from that of which the bulk of the colony formerly consisted. Men of enterprise and industry have been induced to settle in the colony, by the expectation that the abundance of good land which would be granted to them without price, and almost without burdens, would repay the capital and industry engaged on it, better than the highly rented and taxed lands of their native country; or, than any other mode of investing their capital, and employing their industry, was capable of doing, where it had so much competition to contend with.

The number of the respectable portion of the community has also been increased, by the families and descendants of the original and successive officers of the military and civil establishments, who, pleased with the fineness of the climate, and, perhaps, influenced by motives similar to those of the emigrants, have relinquished the desire of returning home, for the prospects offered by a settlement in the colony; and lastly, by many of the reformed convicts, and their children, whose conduct entitles them to be considered respectable members of society.

The returns of population have, accordingly, for some time, shewn a considerable excess of free persons; and the formation of settlements in the North, for the removal of the convicts not necessary for the service of these, and of the government, with other arrangements, shew, that the interests of the former have become a subject of consideration, independently of the latter; and that the time has arrived, when New South Wales ought to be, and is, considered in a different light from what it was when it consisted only of convicts and their rulers.

Agriculture has been said to be the natural and proper business of all new colonies. But this must have been said with reference to that agriculture, which has for its object the raising of some article of produce, over and above the consumption of the colonists, for exportation to the mother country, or to some other market where the price would afford a profit to the cultivators. Without such exportation, how were the colonists to obtain the numerous articles of manufacture indispensable in civilized life, and the not less numerous articles of luxury, which previous habit had made necessary to their comfort, much less to advance with those rapid strides to wealth and importance, which have, in all ages of the world, been the characteristics of new colonies, planted in favourable situations?

That the situation of the colony of New South Wales has been unfavourable for the exportation of the surplus produce of those articles, to the raising of which, its agricultural industry has hitherto been confined, the late history, and present aspect of its agriculture, furnishes abundant proof.

As long as the demand of government was equal to the surplus produce of the country, the want of a foreign market was not felt; but when the demands of government, though increasing, ceased to bear any proportion to the increased number of cultivators, and it became impossible for each cultivator to dispose of the whole of his surplus produce to the commissariat, it was natural, that in the absence of any other internal market, he should look to another country for that demand which was no longer to be found at home. The distance of Great Britain made it impossible that he should there find a profitable market, even had the war price of agricultural produce continued. The Cape of Good Hope was looked to and tried, but there the competition of the Americans was too powerful for him to obtain a remunerating price; and, as was the natural consequence, his industry was cramped, and his fields left untilled;—nay, according to some accounts, his crops were allowed to perish on the field, because a glut of the market gave him no hopes that its sale would indemnify him for the expence of gathering it.

Perhaps, under any other circumstances, the effect of such an excess of produce, thrown on the markets of the colony, would have been to reduce prices so low as to occasion an indisposition, if not an inability to cultivate the following year, and famine might have followed in the train, and as the consequence of excessive production.

The regulations of the Governor in fixing the prices of produce at a rate which would repay with a profit the expence of production, has, to a great extent, prevented this misfortune, since the colony was capable of supplying itself. But the evils of an uncertain market have, nevertheless, been severely felt, and it is certainly more owing to these, than to either "the uncertainty of climate, "or the carelessness of convict servants, that "the colony has been under the necessity of "importing grain from Van Diemen's Land, "and even more lately from Valparaiso."*

---

* This introduction was written during the passage to the colony, in December 1823. If its principles required illustration or proof, none could be afforded, better than the state of the corn market in the colony since that period. For some months after the harvest of 1823, the price of wheat did not exceed 3s. 6d. or 4s. a bushel, and at that price it was most difficult to find a market for it. It is said, that some of the more distant settlers actually fed their hogs with it. It is at all events certain, that much was wasted. About four or five months before the harvest of 1824, apprehensions of a scarcity began to be entertained; and in the course of six weeks, or two months, large quantities of wheat,

Having such discouragements to struggle with, as well as the competition of the soil and climate of Van Diemen's Land, the superiority of which, for grain crops, has of

---

imported from Van Diemen's Land, sold at 20s. and 21s. a bushel.

The government, who have for some time obtained supplies by tender, were now loudly complained of for not paying a higher price, and supporting the previous artificial system. It is considered in the colony, that 3s. 6d. or 4s. is, under few circumstances, a remunerating price, but though, by paying a higher price than it was possible to procure it for by tender, the price of wheat might have been supported and less waste have taken place. Still, as long as the commissariat did not purchase all the surplus produce of each cultivator, not disposable in the market, the evil could only be imperfectly and temporarily remedied.

The colony has certainly reached that degree of advancement, and the extent of cleared and cultivated land in proportion to the number of inhabitants is so considerable, that the considerations which made it the wisest policy of government to maintain the prices of produce in its earlier stages, have ceased to exist.

At a time, then, when the impolicy of the interference of government, in directing the industry of any class of the community to other channels than those to which the interests of the parties would naturally lead them, has been so generally recognized, and so extensively acted upon by the legislature at home, it is scarcely to be expected by the colonist of New South Wales, that artificial inducements are to be held out to his industry in the form of a bounty on the growth of wheat, even though it were possible so to distribute the benefits of it, that there should be no real or apparent ground for murmuring.

It appears to me, that there is even much room to doubt, whether the payment of a high price, by the commissariat, would be really advantageous to the settler. At no very distant period, the stimulus afforded by it must be withdrawn, and the re-action felt; and its evident tendency, in the meantime, would be to keep the settler from seeking out other objects of industry, and ascertaining the real grounds on which his ultimate prosperity must rest.

For a steady remunerating price of wheat, and, consequently, a regular supply of the market, there can be no hope till some other production of the soil is raised, which shall share with it the

late attracted the greater number of settlers, and enabled them to undersell the farmer of New South Wales, even in his own market; it is not surprising that the raising of grain in the colony should be confined to the richest soils—that lands, which have been exhausted by the carelessness and incompetence of those who cultivated them, have been entirely neglected—and that the capital and industry of the colony should be directed to other channels.

The most considerable of these, and that which seems to possess, for the capitalist, the greatest inducement is sheep stock, for which the climate of the colony has proved favourable in an uncommon degree, and for which its unsettled districts afford an almost unlimited range.

The attention of some individuals has been turned to the coarser manufactures, but the labour employed in these, however convenient to the colony in its present circumstances, is rather a bar to its trade with other countries, as the high price of labour, the want of skill which experience gives, and of improvements which an extensive capital can alone render available, must enhance the industry of the settler, and supply what it has been found incapable of doing, a profitable article of export. And it is probable, that £1000 expended by government in bringing such an article to the notice of the colonist, would be attended with more real and permanent advantage, than £50,000 in bolstering up an artificial price of wheat.

price of the commodities too much, to allow of their being an article of export.

This remark is, of course, not applicable to very coarse and bulky articles, and perhaps is not applicable at all to the colony in its present state, from the difficulty in directing that labour to the raising of produce, exchangeable for these manufactures with a country whose facilities for manufacturing were greater.

Accordingly, the production of fine wool has been stated, by the commissioner of enquiry, Mr. Bigge, to be " the principal, if not " the only source of productive industry " within the colony, from which the settlers " can derive the means of repaying the " advances made to them by the mother " country, or supplying their own demands " for articles of foreign manufacture."

The chief obstacle to the extension of sheep stock, is the expence of transporting the wool to the place of embarkation, from those stations which are at a distance from it. This obstacle must increase in magnitude, with the increase of the flocks and their consequent distance in the interior; and this distance must soon be very great, as the virtual occupation of 9000 acres of land is stated not to enable Mr. M'Arthur to maintain more than 7000 sheep.

The sinking hopes of those, who depended on the tillage of the soil, have been considerably revived by the late permission to distil spirits from grain in the colony; and there cannot be a doubt, that agricultural industry will thence receive a new impulse; but the benefits derivable from this permission, are of a limited nature.

It will, no doubt, increase the demand for grain, and, consequently, its production; and it will have the very important effect of shielding the colonists from, or at least of mitigating the effects of, a failure of crops. It will also render available, within the colony, a part of that capital which was sent out of it for the purchase of foreign spirits; and these, so far as they go, are benefits of the first importance. But the consumption of this spirit is limited to the colony, and, as to a foreign market, is precisely in the same situation with the grain itself.

Its greatest effects will be to increase, in proportion to the number of inhabitants, the quantity of land in cultivation to the extent necessary for supplying this additional produce of spirits. It will enable the colonist to render available his own soil, for a certain portion of his wants which formerly diminished the limited returns which the limited market for his produce afforded. But here its influence will stop, and its advantages will bear no comparison with that employment for labour and capital, the demand for which is unlimited, because the demand for its products is only limited by the power of production.

It will operate on the prosperity of the colony, as those medicines on the human frame, which (the cure being beyond the power of the physician) are administered to alleviate present pain, and protract the period of that dissolution they cannot prevent.

From a consideration of these circumstances, and under a strong impression of the importance to the colony of an increase of its exportable commodities, the compiler of the following work was induced to spend some months in the best wine districts of France, with a view of acquainting himself with the cultivation of the vine for the making of wine, and having the power to ascertain to what extent it might be profitably cultivated in New South Wales.

The result of the investigations which he made, relative to this subject was, a conviction on his mind, that there was the strongest probability, not of its partial success, but of its supplying the great *desideratum* of a *staple article of export*, to which the colonists of New South Wales might be indebted for their future prosperity.

This conviction was founded, in the first place, on a consideration of the profits derived from the cultivation of vineyards, the value which this culture gives to lands favourable for it over those employed in any other species of agriculture, and its importance in the rural economy of countries where it is most generally and extensively established;—in the second place, on the probability that the climate of New South Wales, and many of its soils, at present useless from their sterility, would be favourable for the culture of the vine;—and in the third place, on its being a culture, for the products of which, an extensive market might be found.

In visiting, and attentively observing, some of the most celebrated wine districts in the south of France, the compiler of the following work found every soil, which by its nature or situation was favourable for the cultivation of the vine, exclusively devoted to that purpose; and to many of these it had given a value which made him doubt very strongly of the information he received, though from most respectable sources, till he had an opportunity of confirming its correctness, by the corresponding notes of that acute and accurate observer, Mr. Arthur Young, and by the later work of the Count de Chaptal.

In the neighbourhood of Cadillac, a small town on the right bank of the Garonne, where the compiler for some time resided, a vineyard was for sale, which had been for many years in a state of decay, from the sons of the former proprietor having been in the army at the time of his death, and shewing, on their return home little industry, or inclination to cultivate for their common advantage, what had fallen to them in equal right. Its extent was 40 *journeaux* of Cadillac, which is equal to about 27 and one-third English acres. The buildings on it could not much exceed £100 in value. The price demanded was 45,000 francs, 40,000 had been offered. The medium price 42,500, or £1770 16s. sterling, is £65, or, allowing £100 for buildings, £62 an English acre nearly. At this price, one of the best judges of the country, the mayor of Cadillac, affirmed, that if the purchaser possessed skill and capital to do it justice, it ought to repay him his purchase money in six years, though by that time it could hardly be brought to the high state of cultivation in which it was kept by the father of the present proprietors.

Cadillac is not famous for the quality of its wines, but on the opposite side of the river, Sauterne, Barsac, and Preignac, produce the famous white wines which go by their names; and here, as might be expected, the first soils reach a still higher value. The *Journal* of Barsac contains only a very small fraction more than half an English acre, and yet it cannot be purchased for less than 2,000 francs, or £160 an English acre.

Conversing, one day, with a considerable proprietor, on the value of vineyards, the compiler was informed by him, that on one occasion he had sold the produce of a vineyard in Sainte Croix, of 10¼ acres in extent for 12,000 francs. He acknowledged that a lifetime might elapse before another such vintage would occur, but said that instances were not wanting of a still greater produce; mentioning one near Lafitte, in the district of Medoc, where the best claret wines are made, for which 100,000 francs (£4166 sterling) had been refused, and of which, one year's produce had been known to bring 30,000 francs, and yet this vineyard did not exceed six English acres in extent. Its excessive value was owing to its possessing, in a very uncommon degree, the rare property of producing in large quantities without deteriorating the quality of the produce.

According to Young, the whole district which produces the famous Champagne wines is included in five leagues' length. As an average of the value of vineyards in this district, the price of an acre is stated at 3,000 francs, and the nett annual profit, including rent (for throughout France every proprietor cultivates his own vines), at £14 18s. 4d. sterling, being 10 per cent. on that sum.

In his first work on the vine, pulished in 1801, not very long after Young's tour, the Count de Chaptal states, that when vines are cultivated extensively, and with an abundant capital, they pay from 9 to 12 per cent. on the money expended.

INTRODUCTION.

Young's notes give £61 8s. as the average value of an acre of vines for all France; but, leaving out of his estimate all which exceed £100 in value, and £21 in produce, he fixes the average value of vines in France at £45 an acre; and their gross annual produce at £9 2s. being one-fifth of their fee simple.

By the following table, he shews the proportional value of the produce of vineyards, to that of soils under other culture, and also the proportional rent or profit which they yield.

Gross Produce of the Lands of France.

Arable Land,	70,000,000 acres at	40 francs,	£122,660,563
Vines,	5,000,000	175	38,225,250
Woods,	19,850,000	16	13,895,300
Meadow, and rich pasture,	4,000,000	100	17,500,000
Lucerne, &c.	5,000,000	100	21,875,000
Pastures & Wastes,	27,150,000	10	11,878,125
Total	131,000,000 acres		£226,236,313

Nett Rent, or Profit of the Lands of France.

Arable and Lucerne,	75,000,000 acres at	£0 15s. 7d.	£57,437,500
Woods,	19,850,000	0 12s. 0d.	11,910,000
Vines,	5,000,000	8 16s. 6d.	19,125,000
Meadow,	4,000,000	2 3s. 9d.	8,750,000
Wastes,	27,150,000	0 1s. 9d.	2,375,625
Total,	131,000,000		£99,898,125

Without possessing, of himself, the same ample data which Mr. Young's extensive tour gave him, for determining the value of an acre of vines at the present day, the compiler is enabled to copy, from the preface to the Count de Chaptal's last work, a table shewing the state of the culture of the vine, and the quantity of wine produced, which he conceives confirms very strongly the truth of Mr. Young's calculation. The prices are fixed at the very lowest prices of commerce, even in years of the greatest abundance.

The extent of soil under the vine in France, as established by the administration of indirect contributions in 1809, was 1,613,939 hectares, and the produce on an average of five years, 35,358,890 hectolitres of wine. The prices as under:—

10,500,000 hectolitres at 7 francs, 50 cents	78,750,000 francs.
4,600,000	10	46,000,000
3,400,000	15	51,000,000
2,300,000	20	46,000,000
2,000,000	25	50,000,000
1,700,000	30	51,000,000
1,600,000	35	56,000,000
1,500,000	40	60,000,000
1,600,000	50	80,000,000
800,000	200	160,000,000
30,000,000 hectolitres		678,000,000 francs.

The remaining 5,358,890 are supposed to be employed in distillation, they are of a middling quality, but taken at the lowest price, 7 francs 50 cents they give 40,191,675, which added to the above, makes 718,941,675 francs.

In 1817, the quantity of land under the vine had increased to 1,977,000 hectares, and the quantity of wine taken at the same rate of increase will be 43,312,991 hectolitres, and its value calculated as before, 880,670,020 francs, or £36,694,584 sterling.

The hectare contains 2·3444 English acres, and the hectolitre 26·49 English gallons, so that the extent of land is 4,634,878, and the quantity of wine 1,147,361,231 gallons, being 247¼ an acre, and at the price of 7·67d, or rather less than 7¼d. a gallon, its gross produce is, £7 18s. 4d. sterling, an acre.

The quantity of land is rather less than it was estimated at by Young, though it has increased since his time, but it was not then ascertained by authority.

"We must not fail to observe," says Chaptal, "that these are the very lowest "prices of wine, even in years of the greatest "abundance, and that the truth would not "be exceeded, were the amount carried to "1,000,000,000 francs." At this price, it comes so very near the estimated produce of Young, that there can be little doubt his calculation of £45 an acre is near the average value of vines in France at present, if the principles on which he establishes the relative value of soils and produce are correct

"To form a correct idea," continues Chap-
" tal, of the advantages France draws from her
" vineyards, it is necessary to take into ac-
" count, that four-fifths of the soil consecrated
" to the vine, would remain uncultivated
" without it. The poorest soils are peculiarly

"adapted for producing good wines, and the most renowned vineyards which are worth, under this culture, from 10,000, to 15,000 francs an arpent,* would be, without it, destitute of value."

At the time Mr. Young made the calculations referred to, he estimated the gross produce of the cultivated land in England, at 50s. an acre. In 1814, Sir John Sinclair estimated the gross produce of cultivated lands in Scotland, at £4 4s; and in 1812, Colquhoun made his estimate of the lands and agricultural property in Great Britain, in which he fixes the average value of an acre of cultivated land at £24 sterling.

The following Table is for England.

Gardens and Nurseries,	20,000 acres at £70		£1,400,000
Lands highly cultivated in the vicinity of large towns,	500,000	50	25,000,000
Hop grounds	100,000	40	4,000,000
Lands cultivated, of a superior quality,	12,000,000	30	360,000,000
Lands cultivated, of an inferior quality,	18,000,000	20	360,000,000
			£750,400,000

Uncultivated lands and wastes in England and Wales 6,714,400, acres at £15.

It will be seen by the above table, that only a very few lands favoured by their situation, bear any comparison in value with the vineyards of France; what then are we to

---

* The arpent of France, contains 1·185, or 1 and 1-5th English acres nearly.

think of that culture, which gives to such a vast extent of the *waste lands* of a country, a value not attained by the richest soils of other countries where the climate is unfavourable for it, with the exception of a very few in favourable situations?

It is not surprising that so lucrative a branch of rural economy, and one which, besides the internal and foreign commerce it gives rise to (decidedly the most extensive of any in France), is understood to yield to the government of the country, a revenue at least as much exceeding that derived from any other branch of agricultural industry, as the profits of vineyards to the proprietors exceed those of other soils, should be considered as one of the very first sources of the wealth of France; and that its improvement should be considered of the first importance. Accordingly, in the latter half of the last century, upwards of thirty French writers have published works on the improvement of the cultivation of the vine, and the making of wine.

The compiler is not aware to what extent, in other wine countries, this subject has employed the pens of scientific men; nor has he had any opportunity of ascertaining its relative importance in their rural code; but if it be true, as has been said, that fifteen-sixteenths of the vineyards of Portugal are cultivated with British capital, and that the same is the case, to a certain extent, with those of Sicily;

it may reasonably be concluded, that these capitals were not invested in the soil of a foreign land, without the certainty of a very handsome return: and that it is not in France alone that the vine is a source of wealth.

With regard to climate and soil. Those climates which are favourable for the culture of the vine in the northern hemisphere, are found to lie between the 50th and 35th degree of latitude; and it is between these parallels that the most famous wines are produced. The latitude of a great part of New South Wales is within the 35th degree, but when the difference of temperature at the same degree of latitude in the two hemispheres is considered, it will be found to correspond nearly with those countries which are in the middle of the vinous latitudes of the north. A proof of the fitness of the climate might also be urged, in the success which has attended the introduction of the fruits of wine countries, and even of the grape itself; though many climates bring the grape to perfection as a fruit for the table, which nevertheless do not impress upon it the characters peculiar to those grapes, from which good wines are made. But, the Cape of Good Hope is in the same latitude* as New South Wales, and

---

* The compiler is aware that other circumstances, besides mere position on the surface of the globe, must be considered as forming climates: but, he conceives that these circumstances as relating to New South Wales, are not sufficiently ascertained to allow of any thing being founded upon them.

the Cape possesses the vineyards of Constantia, than which, we need not go farther for proofs of the suitableness of the climate for the production of the finest wines, or the capacity of vineyards, when favourably situated and cultivated with care, for enriching their owners.

Of the fitness of soil, perhaps nothing can be said here more to the purpose than one of the concluding sentences of that section of the first chapter, which treats on soils. "From what has been said, it may be concluded, that the vine may be advantageously cultivated in a great variety of soils. The conclusion may even be drawn, that the intrinsic nature of the soil is of less importance, than that it should be porous, free, and light."

With regard to a market for the produce, the distance of Great Britain from the colony might, at first sight, encourage the belief that wine would not bear the expence of conveyance to that country, and perhaps this might be true of inferior wines; but, besides that, these could be converted into brandies New South Wales possesses, from its situation, peculiar advantages, in competing with those countries which supply the Indian market, for which, as appears by the evidence before the House of Lords on foreign trade, the demand was never so great as of late.

And perhaps it might be worthy of consideration, in a national point of view, to what extent the advantages, which, during the war, Great Britain derived from London being the depot of many thousand tons of wines, destined for the Indian and other markets; and by the carrying trade* of those wines which her shipping then enjoyed, might be restored to the country, by the successful cultivation of the vine in New South Wales. Its first effects would be, that the ships which go out with convicts and emigrants would obtain a freight home; or, instead of going in ballast to seek a return cargo in India, might carry thither a cargo of wines. From this it would result, that government might obtain ships for the transportation of convicts at a cheaper rate, and that emigrants might obtain a cheaper passage with equal profit to the ship owners.

It were superfluous to go about to prove, that an extensive and profitable investment for capital, and employment for labour, would increase the resources of the colony, and consequently its intercourse with Great Britain;— that, in its altered circumstances, it would present a more extended, and increasing, market for her manufactures;—and that the bond of union, between the colony and the

---

* See evidence of C. L. Tavernier, John Hall, and John Gowan, Esquires, in the Report of the House of Lords, on Foreign Trade, (Silk and Wine Trade), ordered by the House of Commons to be printed, 1821.

mother country, would be strengthened by the colonists having the means of employing their industry, and the advantages of their climate in a way not interfering with the mother country in her manufactures or commerce; but which, while it afforded new channels for the latter, would make it their interest to prefer her manufactures to those which, in their present circumstances, are springing up among themselves.

That the cultivators of the Cape have not succeeded, in any considerable degree, in producing wines to the taste of Indian consumers, is no reason why those of New South Wales should be unsuccessful, *tot vina quot agri*, says Pliny, who, among other illustrious men of ancient times, treated of this subject; and this is a truth, which the extension of the vine over Europe, has only more extensively proved: and it is not less true, that the differences of cultivation and management, produce as great diversities in the wine, as the differences of soil and situation. The first planters of the Cape, came from a country, the very reverse in its nature of one fit for the culture of the vine; and it is natural to suppose, that many of them, ignorant of its cultivation, applied to it the maxims of an agriculture, which might be excellent for raising corn crops on the damp and rich soils of Holland, but which, when applied to the culture of the vine on the hills of the Cape, were the very reverse of those by which a cultivator, well acquainted with the subject, would be guided.

The wine *boers* of the Cape have, besides, been accused of carelessness in the making of their wines, and the distillation of their brandies; and to one, who is acquainted with the peculiar care and management in the cultivation of the plant, which is necessary to preserve the most advantageous proportion among the different vegetable principles in the fruit, and with the solicitude with which the fermentation of the best wines, and the distillation of the best brandies is conducted, it ceases to be a matter of surprise, that the generality of Cape wines, made under such circumstances, are so much inferior to those of older wine countries.

The greater part of the information contained in the following treatise, is derived from the work of the Count de Chaptal, published at Paris in 1819. The name of Chaptal stands among the highest in general science; to him the world is indebted for many valuable works, and particularly for his " Chemistry applied to the Arts." His country (in which he for some time filled the post of minister of the interior), is under more particular obligations, for the attention he bestowed on the subject of this work, so important to her interest, and which has procured for him there the title of " Legislator of Vinification."

It had been the fault of most preceding writers on this subject, to prescribe, as proper for every soil and climate, a system of management which had been found the best in one particular district. It was the object of Chaptal, to examine the different methods of procedure in different districts, with reference to the general principles of chemical science—to ascertain what was due to the influence of climate, seasons, soil, exposure, and culture on the plant—to explain the nature of each of the substances which is contained in the juice of the grape, and the influence exercised by it on fermentation, and its result; and thence, to deduce general principles, by the application of which, to the circumstances in which he found himself placed, each cultivator wrought from rules for his guidance.

It was the compiler's wish to present, as shortly as possible, in the following pages, the information necessary to enable any person to commence, and conduct, the operations of the vineyard and wine cellar, as far as written instructions were capable of doing so. He has, therefore, abstained from following Chaptal into historical details and disquisitions, not immediately related to the subject in hand. He was also anxious to notice the opinions of contemporary writers where they are different: and lastly, from the generalizing nature of Chaptal's work, he was obliged to have recourse to other authors for practical details not furnished by him: and to his own notes* for some of these, which, to an author writing for the improvement of his subject, might seem superfluous; but which he, considering himself as writing for those who were entirely ignorant of it, could not but deem essential.

He has not, therefore, exactly followed Chaptal's arrangement, and has in many cases used his own language. The important chapters on fermentation, however, are either a liberal translation, or a careful abridgment from his work: and he, therefore, hopes he has avoided any considerable error into which he might have been betrayed, by having but a limited acquaintance with chemistry.

Whatever other errors the work may contain, he trusts that they are not of a nature

---

* The compiler is happy to acknowledge himself indebted to the kindness of a gentleman of high rank in the colony, for the first work of Chaptal, in which, the practical matters here alluded to, are treated in detail by M. Dussieux, of the Society of Agriculture at Paris. He has been, of course, less under the necessity of referring to his own notes, in which, from want of experience, he could not altogether confide. He has, also, in preparing the work for the press, retrenched many notices from various authors, from the necessity of keeping the work in small bounds; and from a persuasion, that most of them might be brought under some one of the general principles established by Chaptal.

seriously to mislead any one who is guided by it; and trusting to the importance of the matter, rather than to the manner in which it is treated, he submits it to the colonists of New South Wales, entreating for it, in the absence of any other English work on the subject, the candid consideration of the advantages which may result from it as it is, to balance the defects, which may distinguish it from what, in abler hands, it might have been.

PART FIRST.

CHAPTER FIRST.

Of the influence of Climate, Soil, Exposure, Seasons, and Culture, on the Vine.

OF all the plants which cover the surface of our globe, there is, perhaps, none more sensible of the action of the numerous causes which influence vegetation, than the vine. Not only do we see it varied under different climates, but even in the same climate, we see its products changed in the most astonishing manner, in consequence of a difference in the nature of the soil, the exposure of the vineyard, or the system of cultivation pursued in it.

Causes which have no perceptible effect on other plants, act so powerfully on this, as to seem to change its nature. In all the wine countries, there are instances of vines of the same variety, cultivated in the same manner, and in contiguous fields, differing more than one-half in value, in consequence of a slight difference in their exposure, or of the slope of the hill on which they are planted.

Were we to judge of the vine, by the strength of its vegetation, or the quality of its fruits, the effects of these causes would be much less perceptible; our senses would frequently establish very slight shades of difference; but, estimating their effects by a comparison of the wines made from these fruits, we are only the more sensible of the differences, as our taste for this beverage becomes more exercised, or refined.

Before, then, we can determine the causes why the same kind of plant does not produce every where, indifferently, the same quality of wine, and establish principles by which we shall be able to foresee and announce that which ought to be, as well as to account for that which is, it is necessary that we should examine, separately and with care, what is due to each of the causes which most strongly influence the vine, and its products.

SECTION I.

Of the Influence of Climate on the Vine.

ALL climates are not favourable for the culture of the vine. If it grows, and seems even to vegetate with force, in the colder climates, it is not less true, that its fruit never attains a sufficient degree of maturity, and it is an observation which constantly holds just, that beyond the 50th degree of northern latitude, the juice of the grape is not capable of undergoing a fermentation, to convert it into an agreeable drink.

The flavour, and especially the saccharine principle of the grape, are effects of the uninterrupted rays of a powerful sun: where the sun's rays are less powerful and constant, the sour or acrid juice, which developes itself in the grape at its first formation, is not sufficiently elaborated, and does not lose its primitive character of greenness, before the return of winter arrests its further progress to maturity.

The unripened grape contains scarcely any sugar, and the expressed juice, when fermented, yields a sour liquor, in which the alcohol scarcely exists in sufficient quantity to impede the movements of a putrefactive fermentation.

The vine, like every other production of nature, has its appropriate climates, and, in general, it is only between the 35th and 50th degrees of northern latitude that it can be cultivated with advantage; if it flourishes at a lower latitude than 35 degrees north, the heat of the climate must be modified by natural causes, as in the Canary Islands, to which the cooling influence of the surrounding ocean, imparts the advantages of a colder clime, or measures must be resorted to for counteracting the influence of a parching atmosphere, as in some parts of Persia, where, by means of irrigation, the vine is said to be cultivated under a temperature, whose mean is, 82 degrees of Fahrenheit.

Vineyards are also to be found, and a little wine is made, as far north as the 52d degree, but on either side of the above boundaries, the wine is of a very inferior character, or requires, for its production, too much expense and care, to be a profitable article of culture. The best wines are made between the 40th and 50th degrees of latitude.

But though the climate impresses a general and indelible character on its productions, there are circumstances which modify its action: and it is only by studying, separately and carefully, the influence of each of these, that we can recognise the effect of climate in all its strength. It is thus, that we sometimes see, under the same climate, very different qualities of wine, because the differences of soil, exposure, or culture, modify the immediate influence of this grand agent.

The influence of climate, is in nothing better illustrated than in the changes which vine plants undergo, when transported to a foreign country, where the same method of culture may be pursued, on a soil of a similar nature, without the wine produced having any analogy to that which they bore on their native soil. Thus, many of the vines at the Cape of Good Hope, are said to have been originally carried out from Burgundy, and none of the Cape wines have any resemblance to those of that province. Most of the wine drank at Madrid is made from stocks originally from the same country.*

History informs us, that vine plants, carried from Greece into Italy, produced no longer the same wine; and that the celebrated vines of *Falernum*, cultivated at the foot of Vesuvius, have changed their nature.

Warm climates, in favouring the production of saccharine matter, generally produce strong spirituous wines, sugar being necessary to the for-

---

* This sentence of Chaptal, of course implies, that the wines alluded to are unlike those of Burgundy. In a topographical account of vineyards, I find the following passage:—

"The principal vineyards of New Castile, are in the southern provinces of La Mancha and Toledo. Their products are very considerable, and in general of a good quality; but the wines they make in the north are all dry, rough, and destitute of body and spirit. A great deal of the wines of La Mancha are sent to Madrid, where the inhabitants, in easy circumstances, use them as common wines, *(vins d'ordinaire)*. They are less coloured, less strong, and, consequently, more delicate than the greater part of Spanish wines. The best are cultivated in the vicinity of Valdepennas, and it is affirmed, that they have an analogy to our good Burgundy wines, of which they unite almost all the qualities."

mation of alcohol; while the wines produced in colder climates, though sometimes agreeably perfumed, are characterized by their want of strength, and tendency to degenerate into the acetous fermentation.

It is, however, contended by some authors[*], that an excess of saccharine matter is a defect in the grape, especially if the wine be intended for the table. Thus, in Burgundy, where the sun's rays do not act so powerfully in the production of saccharine matter, the wines are distinguished by a richness and delicacy of taste and flavour, while those produced under the burning sun of Languedoc and Provence, possessing no virtues but spirituosity, are generally employed in distillation. Not that the existence of a large portion of saccharine matter is incompatible with that of flavour and perfume, but it generally happens, that the volatile principles on which these depend, are dissipated during the lengthened fermentation necessary to convert into alcohol, the excess of saccharine matter.

---
[*] Labergerie, "Cours d'Agriculture."

SECTION II.

Of the Influence of Soil on the Vine.

THE vine grows every where, and were we to judge of the quality of its produce, by the vigour of its vegetation, we should prefer for its culture the most fertile and best manured soils; but experience proves, that the quality of the wine bears little relation to the luxuriance of the plant: perhaps it is not going too far to say, that the excellence of the wine is inversely, as the strength of vegetation shewn by the vine. Nature has reserved for the vine, dry, light, and free soils, and confided to those which are strong the production of corn—

" *Hic segetes, illic veniunt felicius uvæ* "

Rich argillaceous soils are, in all points of view, improper for the vine; their firmness prevents the dissemination of the minute fibres of the roots, and their coldness is prejudicial to the plant. If a light shower falls, it is evaporated before it sinks beneath the surface, and the same coherence, which prevented the entrance of a less degree of moisture, opposes itself to the evaporation of those heavy rains which penetrate deeper. Thus, the root seldom receives moisture but in excess, and the air and heat, finding the same obstacles to their entrance and circulation as the water, a perpetual coldness in the soil checks the vigour of the plant, or an excess of moisture rots its roots, and causes its decay.

There are, however, soils rich in nutritious substances, which, containing a larger proportion of siliceous or calcareous matter, do not partake of the hurtful qualities of those in which argil predominates. In these, the vine grows freely, but this very strength of vegetation, as has been before observed, is essentially hurtful to the quality of the grape, which, with difficulty, attains to maturity, and produces a wine without strength or flavour. If, then, a rich soil is free and open, the vine planted in it flourishes vigorously, producing in abundance a wine, weak, watery, and destitute of perfume; but, in wet and humid soils of every description, it languishes and dies.

Calcareous soils are in general favourable to the vine; dry, free, and light, they every where afford a free circulation to the water with which they are impregnated, and allow the numerous tender ramifications of the roots to extend in all directions, in search of the juices which are appropriated by the plant. Their stimulating nature, too, which, while it increases the energy of the plant, does not impart to it an excess of nutriment, points them out as peculiarly fitted for its culture.

Accordingly, we find the soils of many celebrated vineyards to be calcareous. Some of the best soils of Champagne, rest upon a substratum of chalk, in which the vine is long of coming to maturity; but in which, when once rooted and established, it maintains itself with vigour. Chalk also enters largely into the composition of the soil, which produces the celebrated white wines of Sauterne.

A mixture of stones is always an important addition even to a soil possessing all the requisites of dryness, lightness, and porosity. The root spreads itself easily in a soil rendered penetrable by a mixture of rounded stones, and while the bed of pebbles on the surface oppose themselves to the evaporation of the necessary moisture, they facilitate the filtration of what may be in excess, and reflect back on the grape, the benign influence of the sun's rays.

Volcanic soils have been always observed to produce delicious wines. These virgin soils having been long elaborated in the interior of the earth by subterranean fires, present an intimate mixture of all the earthy principles. When this semivitrified substance is decomposed by the combined action of air and water, it furnishes all the elements of a good vegetation, and the fire with which it is impregnated, seems to pass successively into all the plants confided to it.

Some of the best vineyards of the south of France, are situated on the *debris*, or waste of volcanoes. The decomposed lava at the foot of Vesuvius, produces the famous Italian wine, called Lachryma Christi; Tokay wine is produced on a volcanic soil; and the soil of the hills of Campania, famous for the *Falernum* of the ancients, is said to be coloured yellow, by the sulphur it contains.

There are many places on the varied surface of the globe, where granite has ceased to retain that character of hardness, and indestructibility, which generally distinguishes that primitive rock; and where, pulverized by the action of the elements during many ages, it is reduced to a sand of a finer or coarser description. The soil of the vineyards of Hermitage, and of many others of great celebrity, consists of this decomposed gravel, which seems to possess all the requisites for a superior produce of wine, uniting that lightness and porosity which permits the roots to spread, the water to filtrate, and the air to penetrate, while the stony surface arrests the rays of the sun before they penetrate to the roots.

It may be concluded, from what has been said,

that the vine may be cultivated advantageously in a great variety of soils. The conclusion may even be drawn, that the intrinsic nature of the soil is of less importance, than that it should be porous, free, and light. In Burgundy, a light friable soil, of a reddish or black colour is reputed the best. It has been observed, that the best vineyards of Bordeaux, are on a light, gravelly, and stony soil, partly consisting of decomposed granite: and, when this rests upon a bed of rich sand, it is said to possess the rare property of producing in large quantity, without any deterioration in the quality.

The sandy soil will, in general, produce a delicate wine, the calcareous soil a spirituous wine, the decomposed granite a brisk wine.

When a soil is to be chosen for a vineyard, all cold, compact, and wet soils, and such as are easily hardened by the sun's rays, are to be avoided. If it is more profitable, or desirable, to obtain a large quantity of wine for the general consumption of a country, or for distillation, good rich soils may be resorted to; thus, on the banks of the Cher and Loire, in France, they not only cultivate the vine on rich soils, but even with the aid of manure. But it is an observation, which in general is just, that the soils of the best vineyards are those, which contain little nutritious matter, and four-fifths of the vineyards of France are planted in soils which would not pay the expense of cultivation in another form.

SECTION III

Of the Influence of Exposure on the Vine*.

The same climate, culture, and soils of the same nature furnish, frequently, wines of a very different quality. We daily see a hill covered with vines, afford, under different aspects, the most amazing diversity of produce.

One would imagine that every variety of climate and soil had concurred in furnishing products, which are the natural fruits of contiguous fields differently exposed.

This difference in product, owing to exposure,

---

* It is almost unnecessary to remark, that these observations are only literally applicable in the northern hemisphere. I have preferred stating them as I found them, because the illustrations are all drawn from it, and it will be an easy matter to apply the general principles, which it is the object of this chapter to establish, as far as mere latitude is concerned. They will, of course, in their application to New South Wales, be modified by various circumstances, which it would probably be difficult for even the oldest and most observant resident fully to appreciate.

is apparent throughout the vegetable kingdom. Timber, cut on the northern aspect of a hill, is much less combustible than what grows on a southern exposure. Odorous and savoury plants lose their odour and savour when produced on a rich soil, looking to the north. Pliny has observed, that the timber on the south of the Appenines, was superior to what grew on a different aspect, and every one knows the effects of exposure on leguminous plants, and fruits.

These phenomena, observable in all the products of vegetation, are peculiarly remarkable in the vine. A vine looking to the south, produces fruits which seem of a different nature from those of one looking northwards. Even in a vineyard, having everywhere the same exposure, the greater or less inclination of the surface has its effect in producing modifications in the quality of the wine, while the summit, the middle, and the base of a hill, furnish products entirely different.

The naked summit receives every instant the impression of changes and movements in the atmosphere;—there the winds agitate the plant;—fogs produce there a more constant, and more direct impression,—the temperature of the air is colder, and more variable;—there, also, hoar frosts are more frequent; and all these causes combine in lessening the quantity of fruit, in checking its progress to maturity, and in giving to the wine an inferior character to that of the middle of a hill, which escapes the effects of these agents, or is exposed to them in a limited degree.

The disadvantages of the base, are of a different nature; there the plant flourishes more vigourously in a better soil, but its fruit contains less saccharine matter, and less flavour than in the middle region. The air being more charged with humidity, and the earth with moisture, the grape is more enlarged by the abundance of sap or common fluid furnished to the plant, but its peculiar principles are imperfectly elaborated. When the wine, at the summit of the *Clos Vougeot*, one of the most celebrated vineyards of Burgundy, sells for 600 francs, that of the middle brings 900, and that of the base only 300.

The exposure, most favourable for the vine is between the east and south. Hills sloping to the south, produce, in general, excellent wines, and when they rise, by a gentle elevation from a plain, present the most favourable situation for a vineyard. A flat soil, and one with too great a slope, have each their disadvantages; a gentle inclination presents the most favourable disposition for the water to spread itself, and filter through the whole soil, without losing itself too fast, or being detained too long.

An open exposure is also a point of capital importance,

—————— *apertos,*
" *Bacchus amat colles,* ———."

A good vineyard is seldom found in a close valley, where the plant is exposed to the injurious effects of cold currents of air, or is endangered by sudden gusts of wind; if the bottom of the valley is the course of a river, the situation is still worse, because the fogs and exhalations have a tendency to produce a constant humidity, always hurtful in its effects.

Keeping these principles in view, the differences of opinion among agriculturists, on this point, may be in a great measure reconciled. Some disapprove of situations near a river, for vines, on account of the fogs and agueous exhalations it engenders—while others defend these situations, by asserting the superiority of the wines of the Rhone, the Garonne, the Marne, the Rhine, and many others.—The neighbourhood of a river is only dangerous where the hills rise precipitately from its banks. In every case, where the slope of the hill rises gradually, and forms an open and extensive valley, not shaded from the rays of the sun, and not liable to be enveloped in the fogs which frequently rise from the beds of rivers, their neighbourhood is, at least, indifferent.

An eastern exposure, though favourable to the vine, is less so than one to the south, as it is generally observed, that vines looking to the east, are more injured by frost. The rays of the rising sun striking suddenly on the tender leaves and flower of a plant, frozen during a cold night, has the effect of burning and destroying them, in the same manner as mortification is the consequence of exposing to a sudden heat, a limb which has been frost-bitten*.

---

* It is remarkable, that English gardeners prefer an eastern exposure, for reasons the very reverse of the above. "An open aspect to the east," says Abercrombie, in his Practical Gardener, "is itself a point of capital importance in laying out a "garden or orchard, on account of the early sun. When the sun "can reach the garden at its rising, and continue a regular in-"fluence, increasing as the day advances, it has a gradual and "most beneficial effect in dissolving the hoar frost which the "past night may have scattered over young buds, leaves, and "blossoms, or setting fruit. On the contrary, when the sun is "excluded from the garden till about ten in the morning, and "then suddenly darts on it with all the force derived from con-"siderable elevation, the situation is bad, particularly for fruit-"bearing plants in the spring months; the powerful rays of "heat at once melt the icey particles, and immediately acting "on the moisture thus created, scald the tender blossom, which "drops as if nipped by a malignant blight."

In this, there seems to me to be no contradiction, but what may be accounted for by difference of climate.

The suns in England, seldom rises free from clouds, and never

A northern exposure has always been considered the most unfavourable, as the vine, from being most exposed to cold and moist winds, is most subject to injury from frosts and fogs, and the grape seldom attains its maturity, where it enjoys, in a small degree, the rays of the sun.

A western exposure is little favourable for the vine. The heat of the day has already dried up all moisture from the soil, when the evening sun, darting his oblique rays under the foliage, scorches and withers the fruit, stopping its vegetation before it has attained its full growth, and inducing a premature ripeness. It is the more unfavourable, that the grape, dried and heated by the last rays of the sun, passes suddenly to a temperature cold and moist; and, that the juices dilated by the heat, and spread through the whole plant, are there fixed, coagulated, and frequently frozen instantaneously.

In Champagne, there is a difference of value, of

---

possesses at his rising, the same power as in wine countries; consequently, the change from cold to heat is not so sudden. While the temperature of the atmosphere, which, in wine countries, is high enough to melt the frost, and gradually dilate the vessels contracted by it, after the sun rises, though his direct rays are excluded, is too low to have the same effect in England, and hence the injury sustained by the increased strength of his rays.—

one-third, between a soil of the same quality, exposed to the south, and one exposed to the west.

Even in a vineyard, situated with every advantage of exposure, nothing should be allowed to interrupt the direct action of the mid-day sun, which, of all causes contributing to the perfection of the grape, is certainly the most powerful. The practice of planting fruit trees in a vineyard, is hence disapproved of, though in some districts it is conceived that they are advantageous in protecting the vines from the effects of frost; and from this idea it is quite common to see the peach, the olive, the apple, and the walnut trees, planted in vineyards. In many districts, also, where, from other causes, the wine is, at the best, of an indifferent quality, they are planted solely on account of their fruit. The least dangerous, are the peach and the olive.

It may be concluded, from what has been said, that the most favourable exposure of the vine is towards the south; and that an eastern, though inferior to a southern exposure, is preferable either to one to the west, or to the north; the vine which enjoys the greater portion of the sun's rays being that which, with equal soil and culture, will generally produce the best wine.

If, in the immense variety of vineyards which cover a portion of Europe, there are exceptions to this rule, it is when the culture and soil supply the defect of exposure, and are directed to the production of a wine which derives its excellencies from qualities independent of spirituosity; but the principle established is strictly just, when the object of cultivation is to obtain that perfect maturity of the grape, and developement of its saccharine principles, which alone form the base, and the character of a perfect grape.

SECTION IV.

Of the Influence of the Seasons on the Vine.

From the principles which have been established, in treating of the effects of climate, soil, and exposure on the vine, it naturally follows, that the season impresses a character on its produce, as it may be distinguished for cold or heat, for humidity or dryness. Accordingly, it is found that a cold and rainy season, in a climate naturally warm and dry, produces on the grape the same effect as a colder climate.

The vine delights in heat, and the grape only attains to perfection in a dry soil, struck by the rays of an ardent sun. When a rainy season induces a constant humidity in the ground, and maintains a damp and moist temperature in the atmosphere, the grape neither acquires such a nice principle nor flavour, and the wine made from it is weak and insipid. These descriptions of wine keep with difficulty; the minute proportion of alcohol which they contain, is insufficient to prevent their decomposition, and the large proportion of that principle, which is the yeast of the fermentation, accelerates the movements of an incipient degeneration; all wines of this description contain a large portion of malic acid, from which they derive a peculiar taste, a sourness which is not acetous, and which impresses a character the more marked, as the wines are less spirituous.

The influence of the seasons is so well known in the wine countries, that the nature of the wine can be predicted long before the period of the vintage. When the season is cold, the wine is generally rough and ill tasted: when wet, the wine is in large quantity, but weak, and though producing little spirit, is usually (at least in the south of France), employed in distillation, both on account of its wanting durability, and those qualities which recommend it as a drink.

The rains which fall at the period, or the approach of the vintage, are always the most dangerous, as the grape has then neither time nor vigour to elaborate the juices with which it is impregnated, and presents, for fermentation, a liquor which is too fluid, and holding in solution too little saccharine matter to produce a strong good bodied wine.

The rains which fall at the moment of the flowering, are also to be dreaded, from their tendency to cause the running of the parts of fructification, and the imperfection of the fruit. But those genial showers, which fall when the fruit begins to enlarge, furnish to the plant the principal elements of its organization, and if heat follows to facilitate the elaboration of these elements, the grape can hardly fail to reach perfection. The most favourable weather for the grape, is that which gives an alternation of heat, and gentle showers.

High winds are always prejudicial to vines; they parch the stocks, the fruit, and the soil, and produce, especially on strong soils, a hard and compact crust at the surface, which prevents the free circulation of the air and water, and keeps an injurious dampness at the root.

The influence of fogs is, in many points of view, injurious to vines; besides the putrid miasm they too often deposit on the fruits of the field, they moisten the surface of the plant, without penetrating farther; and when struck by the rays of the sun, their evaporation is instantaneous. Such sudden changes are always prejudicial to plants, and from the sensibility of the vine, are peculiarly so to it. The injury is still more severe, when, as frequently happens, they are followed by hoar frosts, its extent being in proportion to the degree of moisture congealed, and to the quickness of its evaporation. When such occur, during the critical season of the vines flowering, they generally prove fatal to the hopes of the year, but their effects are to be dreaded by the fruit at all seasons.

Although heat is necessary to ripen the grape, and to furnish it with sugar, it would be an error to imagine that heat alone is capable of producing these desirable properties. It can be but considered, as the agent, in elaborating the juices with which the earth is supposed to be impregnated in sufficient quantity. There must be heat, no doubt, but that heat must not spend itself on a parched soil, in which case, it would scorch rather than vivify.

The good condition of the vine, and the perfection of its fruit, are the effects of a just proportion;—of a perfect equilibrium between the water which furnishes aliment to the plant, and the heat which alone gives to it the power of elaborating that aliment, and extracting from it those principles which constitute the excellence of wines.

SECTION V.

Of the Influence of Culture on the Vine.

Notwithstanding—that a concurrence of so many favourable circumstances, with regard to soil, exposure, and seasons, is necessary to bring the grape to that degree of perfection which, with proper management, insures a good wine; the vine, in climates favourable for it, is a hardy plant.

Though the vines, which now cover a portion of Europe, came originally from the warmer climates of Asia, and spreading gradually through Greece and Italy, accompanied the blessings of civilization, and the amelioration of climate to the western states; the vine is indigenous in many parts of Europe, and in all the climates suited to its nature in both hemispheres in the new world. In Carolina and Florida, wild vines cover the ground in all directions, and are frequently an impediment to the traveller, by entangling his horse's feet in their branches, which in some places trail along the ground, and in others overtop the highest trees. In the wilds of New Holland, also, there is a kind of vine indigenous to the soil.

But, though the vine is thus the spontaneous production of nature, the art of man is requisite to bring it to perfection. Like other fruits and plants cultivated in our gardens, the fruit of the cultivated vine seems of a different nature from that which grows wild in the fields. The influence of culture even extends to compensate, in a certain degree, the defects of climate, as the cultivated grape attains its maturity in a higher latitude by seven degrees, than where the wild vine ripens its austere and diminutive fruit.

Varied as the vine is, by so many natural causes, it is not surprising that it should also be sensible to the effects of culture. A vine of an excellent variety, abandoned to itself, would produce an enormous quantity of grapes the first year, but they would with difficulty ripen, and their quality would be inferior. The following year it would send out more numerous and more feeble shoots, and the fruit would be increased in proportion, but in the same proportion also would its size be diminished—year after year would alter its qualities, till nothing remained to distinguish it from the wilding of the hedge.

To prevent this degeneration, it is necessary that it should be pruned, and the manner of pruning the vine has its influence on the wine. The greater the number of branches left on a stock, the greater will be the abundance of grapes, but the more inferior will be the quality of the wine, and the shorter will be the period of the vine's life.

But, besides pruning the luxuriance of the plant, and preventing it from wasting its strength in large quantities of fruit and foliage, it is necessary, as happens in few other cases*, that nutritious substances should be sparingly supplied to it. Manures which are so necessary to most plants, and especially to those cultivated for their farinaceous matter, are injurious here. It is true, they add to the vigour of vegetation, but they debase the quality of the wine. Accordingly, we find that, in some wine districts, the use of dung was prohibited by law. The reputation of the wine was considered public property. "By public decree," says Olivier de Serres, "the use of dung was forbid at Gaillac, lest it should hurt the character of their white wines with which they supplied their neighbours of Toulouse, Montauban, Cas-

---

* It is observed, in the West Indies, that when sugar plantations are richly manured, the quantity of sugar produced is large, but the quality is inferior. It is for this reason that the sugars of the rich alluvial soils of Demerara are so much inferior to those of Barbadoes, which grow on a soil more exhausted. It is also observed, that the berry of the West India coffee produces two large seeds, while the coffee plant of Arabia yields only one small seed in the berry. West India coffee grows on richly manured soils, while that of Arabia grows on a poor and meagre soil; but though much inferior in size and produce, it is infinitely superior in the flavour, for which coffee is valued.

" tres, and other places, and thus deprive them of
" a trade, from which they drew the most considerable part of their revenues."

As, however, circumstances which can only be
estimated by each proprietor, sometimes makes it
advantageous to plant vines on good soils, with a
view to obtain a larger quantity of wine, though of
an inferior quality, so with the same views it is by
no means uncommon to assist poor soils by the
addition of manure.

Indeed, in some countries the pruning knife is
so sparingly applied, and the soil where it grows
so rich, that the vine seems to change the character of a shrub for that of a tree. Travellers
speak with rapture, of bowers formed by the vine,
intertwining itself with, and overtopping the highest branches of, the olive and the mulberry;—of
the delightful shade of their contrasted foliage, and
the refreshing coolness of their delicious fruit;— of
the richness of that soil, which, in addition to
these, can bear heavy crops of wheat in the intervals of their festooned rows; —and of the benignity
of that clime, where the husbandman sees the
same field " run o'er" with the gifts of Ceres and
Bacchus, and with the " amber store" of the olive,
or the mulberry, from whose leaves the silk worm
draws its delicate thread, to administer to his
luxury and pride.

Of such a nature are the descriptions of more than one traveller through Lombardy, and other parts of Italy, and few could visit the same scenes without participating in the feelings by which they were dictated. Prospects of a similar nature also greet and delight the traveller in many provinces of Spain, and even in the most southern districts of France, the vine is found embracing the branches of the elm and the almond, and hanging its clusters from their highest tops. But it is not in scenes like these that the vine sheds its richest juice—not all the bunches which hang in profusion from these lofty trees enjoy the maturing influence of the sun's rays, and such as reach maturity, are universally found to be destitute of those principles which fermentation converts to a generous wine.

It is thus possible by culture, to raise the creeping vine above the highest trees; nay, to change its twisted and deformed stock, to a noble trunk, which will vie in longevity with the venerable oak. Evelyn informs us, from Theophrastus, of a vine, "which had grown to that bulk and "woodiness, as to make a statue of Jupiter, and "columns in Juno's temple, and that, at present, "it is found that the great doors of the cathedral "at Ravenna are made of such vine tree planks, "some of which are twelve feet long, and fifteen

"inches broad; the whole of that country pro-
"ducing vines of a prodigious growth. Such
"another in Margiana, is spoken of by Strabo,
"that was twelve feet in circumference, and Pliny
"mentions one of 600 years old in his time.

Vines of such an age and stature, may form an attraction to the naturalist, and the traveller may forget his weariness in the bowers formed by their intermarriage with the olive, but the wine which is best calculated to make glad his heart, is the production of a stinted shrub, and a meagre soil.

Accordingly, the cultivation of the best vineyards is directed, not only to reduce the luxuriance of the plant, but to allow that which remains a scanty nourishment, and to suffer it to bear only such a quantity of fruit, as it is found capable of elaborating to the highest degree of perfection.

The practical details by which the principles established in the foregoing pages, are applied in pursuance of this object, form the subject to be treated of in a succeeding chapter.

CHAPTER SECOND.

Of Varieties of Vines, and their Propagation by Seed.

THOUGH, botanically speaking, there is but one species of the wine yielding vine, *(vitis vinifera)* because the specific characters are such only as are always renewable by seed, yet the differences among its varieties are so great, as to make a notice of these not the least interesting, or important part of a treatise on their culture.

It is, however, a division of the work on which I enter with the greatest diffidence, not only on account of the diversity of opinions I find among the French writers[*], but of the unsatisfactory conclusion to which they all appear to me to have come.

It seems to be now agreed among botanists, that " the only genuine reproduction of the species " of plants, is by seed; all plants propagated by " cuttings, layers, or buds, having a determinate

---

[*] I have met with none who have treated of it at a later date, than that of the first work of Chaptal, Dussieux, &c. (1801).

" existence, in some of a shorter, in others of a
" longer period; but that these last methods have
" the advantage of perpetuating the peculiar qua-
" lities of the individual or variety."*

It would be difficult to reconcile to this principle, the facts which history and observation afford us respecting the vine. In all the notices which history has left us, of its introduction into France, and its culture in that country, as well as in those which carry us back to the ages of fable, in Italy and Greece; there is, as far as I have been able to find, no mention of the propagation of the vine by seed. The materials, indeed, from which our information is derived, are scanty and obscure, but it is remarkable, that at this day, the unlettered vigneron of France, is scarcely aware that it is possible by this method to propagate the plant; and those who treat scientifically of the subject, rather mention it as a fact, which could not well be omitted, than one, from which useful results might be obtained.

The French writers have never, therefore, referred to their propagation by seed, the numerous varieties of vines which at this day cover a portion of Europe; nor, indeed, does it appear to be necessary, for daily experience shows, that to effect

* Smith's Intr. Bot.

a change in the physical appearance of the vine, and still more, in the qualities of its fruits; it is only necessary to change the circumstances in which it is placed, as regards climate, or soil and situation.

It has been already said, that Europe is indebted to Asia for the vine. It would, perhaps, have been more correct to say, for its culture. The Phenicians brought the knowledge of this into Greece, and the Grecian Archipelago; and afterwards into Sicily and Italy, in both which countries it is reported to have previously grown wild*. In the time of Romulus, it had made little progress: but, under the fostering protection of Numa, vineyards were extended, and wines produced in abundance throughout the Roman territory. In the time of Domitian, it had made considerable progress in France†, for it was one of the acts which marked the imbecility and ignorance of this tyrant‡, to order the destruction of all the vineyards of Gaul, because a deficiency in the crops of grain had been attended with a superabundant vintage; as if there were any ana-

---

* See Gibbon's Decline and Fall of the Roman Empire, vol, 1.
† Gibbon supposes that the vineyards of Burgundy are as old as the age of the Antonines.
‡ Montesquieu.

logy between the two families of plants; or, as if the best soil for wine had not been in those days, as well as now, (at least in France), improper for corn.

After being for two centuries deprived of the blessing, it was to the emperor Probus that the Gauls were indebted for liberty to replant the vine; and this era is important, because to it the French writers refer the origin of the most marked distinctions, which form what they call the *families, races,* or *species* of their vines.—" The " plants brought anew through the channels of " commerce, from Sicily and Greece, from the " Archipelago, and the coasts of Africa, became " the types of those innumerable varieties, which, " even to this day, people the vineyards of " France."

Towards the close of the last century, when the light of science, which in France had so long beamed on objects less important to mankind, began to shed a few scattered rays upon that art, which is, in some degree, the basis of all others; and men of genius began to think, that philosophy, without compromising her dignity[*], might co-operate with practical experience, in illustrating the business of the husbandmen, it is not surpris-

---

[*] Notre molesse orgueilleuse, dans le sein des pompes et du luxe

ing, that so interesting and important an article as the vine, should have attracted particular attention.

It was to the improvement of this branch of agriculture, that the attention of the Abbé Rozier, (the Sinclair of France), was in a particular manner directed; and had not his career been cut short, there is every reason to believe, that his practical experience*, directed as it was, by scientific knowledge, would have left his countrymen less to enquire for on this subject.

The idea had occurred to him, of forming an establishment, in which should be brought together all the varieties of vines existing in France. By a comparison of these, he proposed to discover how many differed in character, and how many, only in name—how many possessed properties essentially different, *les essences veritablement differentes*—and in how many, the slight differences which distinguished them from others of the species

---

de villes, attache malheureusement une idée basse à ces travaux champêtres et au détail de ces arts utiles que les maitres et les législateurs de la terre cultivaient de leurs mains victorieuses. Voltaire "*discours de réception à l'académie.*"

* During the many years in which he was engaged on his voluminous work on agriculture, he resided on his paternal estate, and is said never to have recommended any change, of which he had not practically ascertained the advantage.

under which they might be ranked, would disappear when cultivated under the same circumstances with them. This knowledge, when obtained, was to be made the foundation of more extensive, and more useful experiments. He proposed to subject each species to a course of experiments, on soils of a different description; and when the soil, which each particularly affected, and the culture most suitable for it, were thus determined,—to ascertain the degree of fermentation which each species required; what description of wine would result from them separately; what combinations of them would yield a wine of superior goodness and durability; and finally, what species furnished the best brandy, and in the greatest quantity.

This was not merely a project, for its author had proceeded a certain length in forming such an establishment, but the aspect of the times was unfavourable: the revolution which was then breaking out, did not confine its ravages to the crowded city, but made its shock to be felt in the remotest village, and it numbered the Abbé Rozier among its victims.

Another attempt, on the same plan, was made by a different individual, but was carried to no greater length; and even the Society of Natural History of Bordeaux, failed in carrying into execution the same undertaking, of which they had published the prospectus. These failures were probably owing to the intricacy of the subject, and the extensive details it involved; but, at the time the question was agitated, it was the opinion of many, that it would have failed in affording such extensive data as Rozier anticipated. Duchesne, the professor of botany and agriculture, in the Dept. of Seine and Oise, conceived[*], that from the known effects of climate, results obtained at Bordeaux, would offer nothing conclusive for the vineyards of the north, and that it would be necessary to have at least four establishments, if not one in each province, before any thing satisfactory respecting the effects of climate, on the qualities of the grape could be determined. He, however, allowed that Rozier's first object, that of forming a new nomenclature of varieties, might be obtained by the means he proposed.

The opinion of the authors of Chaptal's first work, is in accord with that of Duchesne, as to the effects of climate on the qualities of the produce of the vine; but they think, too, that these effects are so powerful on its physiology, as to make an equal number of establishments necessary to obtain a *synonymie*, on which a new nomenclature might be founded.

---

[*] Annales d'Agriculture, Tom ii. page 420.

A collection of the vines of France has, however, under the administration of Chaptal, since been made, and there are now in the nursery of the Luxembourg, no fewer than 1400 different varieties, of which, 1000 are so distinct, as to merit a particular description.

It was thus, not without reason, that he and his colleagues, in the first work on the vine, should have considered, as chimerical, any attempt to procure in one province the wines of another, by the transplantation of the varieties which produced them. " No plant," say they, " is so sub-
" ject to vary in its forms, and the quality of its
" products, as the vine. It is, in fact, so fickle in
" its characters, that a difference in the heat of the
" atmosphere, in the nature of the soil, or in the
" exposure, suffices in causing such modifications,
" as to make it difficult of recognition in its forms
" or qualities. Why, besides, seek from a dis-
" tance the plants which you have so near at
" hand? For there exists not any wine district in
" France, in which are not found collected, all the
" varieties which you wish to obtain elsewhere.
" They may neither have, it is true, the same name,
" nor the same taste, nor the same qualities. What
" imports it? They are there, notwithstanding.
" If it is by the effect of their degeneration, or
" regeneration, that they cannot be recognised,

"you may expect the same changes on those new
"individuals you would introduce; you will ex-
"perience, in this respect, what has been the
"experience of a thousand others before you.
"Among numerous examples, the following is
"cited in preference, because the place whence
"the proprietor drew his plants of choice, is at no
"great distance from that, where he judged pro-
"per to replant them; and this is a circumstance
"worthy of attention.

"In 1774, the Count de Fontenoy, a proprietor
"in Lorraine, happy in being born with a taste
"for useful projects, and with wealth to make
"costly experiments, formed the design of estab-
"lishing a vineyard of Champagne, on his land of
"Champigneul; several observers, uselessly, re-
"presented to him, that the soil not being that of
"Champagne, he would only obtain the wine of
"Lorraine. The plants were obtained from the
"hill of Rheims, and planted on a slope, with a
"most happy exposure; no care, no expence was
"spared, either in the plantation, or culture, of
"this young vineyard: and the first fruits, in fact,
"seemed to give some promise of success. They
"had a different taste from those of the neighbour-
"ing vineyards, but after seven or eight years, this
"particular taste disappeared, and twenty years

"afterwards, the vines were only distinguished by bearing the name of the plant of Rheims."

Though Rozier, perhaps, expected too much from his experiments, it can hardly be doubted, that were an accurate analysis made, of the soil and subsoil of the best vineyards, the exact bearings of their exposure taken, and a meteorological journal kept in them for a few years;—together with an exact account of the course of cultivation pursued, and the management of the fermentation, France might be able to carry her choice wines, to a much larger proportion than one thirty-fifth of her whole produce, to which they are at present confined.

But, however beneficial such experiments and establishments might prove, in a public point of view, the individual planter would probably find his advantage in following the steps which experience has shewn, to lead to a certain degree of success, rather, than in pursuing novel and expensive measures, in the uncertain expectation of a more valuable return.

The substance of what the French writers have said on this point, amounts to this:—You have, already, extensive and excellent vineyards, and in the lapse of ages, each variety has found out the soil and situation which fits it best, or has found out the soil and situation which fits it best, or has become naturalized to the climate and soil where it grows. Choose your plants from the best in your own neighbourhood, attend to their cultivation, and to the fermentation of your wine, and you will have the best your land is capable of producing.

Now, though the correctness of this reasoning may be questioned, the conclusion to which it leads, is most probably the safest; for though great improvements might, by judicious transplantation, be effected in the French vineyards, the expense and uncertainty may be so great, as to make it not the interest of a private individual to attempt them. But the situation of the planter of New South Wales is different, and it is for his assistance that this work is intended. It becomes important, then, to examine whether the wines of New South Wales may not owe much of their future excellence to the nature of the grapes introduced, and if so, how far we can establish principles to guide us in the choice.

However satisfactory, then, the reasonings of the French writers may appear, when addressed to the planter of a country where the vine has been cultivated for two thousand years, before it can restrain us from endeavouring to obtain, by transplantation, those kinds of grapes which are celebrated for their produce in other countries, it must first be proved, that all the varieties of the *vitis vinifera* are the progeny of one parent stock,—that the modifications which each variety has undergone, and which constitute it, are altogether the effects of circumstances;—and, that each kind, placed under such circumstances, would acquire the same qualities which that parent stock, or any other variety the progeny of it, would in the same circumstances have acquired. But the very use which these writers make of the words *essences, races, varieties,* &c. point out differences of greater or less importance. Now, though our information is not sufficiently exact, to ascertain what are the most fickle characters of the vine, it is evident, from the efforts which have been made, to reduce the subvarieties under certain heads, that there are certain characters peculiar to some which may be traced, where great changes in other respects have taken place; and in the description given, of the principal varieties of the vines of France, in Chaptal's first work, the words *essences primitives,* and *caracteres constant,* intimate in the strongest manner, that all the qualities of a variety are not equally affected by circumstances, if they do not point to a period, when the varieties were few, but the characters distinct. The strongest proof, however, exists, that whatever may have been the origin of the different varieties of vines; some of them have through ages retained characters which distinguished them from others. Modern physiologists still discover, in more than one kind, the characters under which they were described by Columella and Baccius; and the distinction they observed, of a species possessing a leaf covered with a downy or cottony substance, still forms the prominent characteristic of a variety of vines.

There are many facts, also, to prove, that the excellencies of one species may be transferred, not only to different provinces, but to countries immensely distant, provided there is a similarity in the climate. In 1420, the wines of Cyprus were reputed the best in the world. The Portuguese introduced the plants from which they were made, into the island of Madeira, and the Malmesey of that island is its produce. It was carried, by Pedro de Ximenes, into Spain, where it yields the Malaga; and enters largely into the composition of the best wines of that country. In imitation of these examples, Francis I. of France planted two extensive vineyards at Fontainbleau and Concy, with plants brought directly from Greece, but these are now indistinguishable among the common vines of the country.

Different kinds of the muscat are also to be

found in most wine countries, where the temperature is sufficiently high, and the wines made from its produce are universally esteemed; and there are varieties of grapes, which may be traced through the finest vineyards for their excellence, while others are only found where the wines are of no reputation.

While, then, there is no certainty of obtaining the same qualities in a vine after its transplantation, there is still sufficient probability of its not degenerating, to make the trial well worth while; and, while it is of great importance to obtain valuable varieties, it is perhaps still more important, to obtain with them, a knowledge of the circumstances in which they were valuable. By assimilating to these, as much as possible, the circumstances of their new situation, the excellencies of many may be retained, while others may acquire characters for which they were not formerly distinguished; and varieties may arise, capable of producing a wine different in its character from any hitherto made, and as much distinguished for excellence as for novelty.

But these observations only apply to the propagation of the plant, by layers, cuttings, or buds, for it appears evident to me, that the extreme longevity of the vine, and the discovery of various methods of lengthening the periods of its existence, by cutting it down close to the roots, &c. had led the French cultivators altogether to overlook its propagation by seed: and, since the date of the works which have occasioned these observations, the experiments of our countryman, Mr. Knight, on the apple, have unfolded principles respecting the propagation of plants, whose application has already enriched the cider counties of England, with many new and most valuable varieties of that fruit: and for the application of which, to the vine, there is the strongest grounds founded on the general analogy between plants, to warrant an expectation of the most valuable results.

In prosecuting the experiments, detailed in the treatise which he has published on the apple and pear*, this eminent physiologist seems to have kept constantly in view, the analogy between the animal and vegetable kingdoms.

"The effects of cultivation," says he, "on the
"animal and vegetable systems, are extremely
"similar. A change in form, in colour, in size,
"or stature, takes place in each; and in each,
"these changes appear to arise from similar

---

* See "A Treatise on the Culture of the Apple and Pear, and on the Manufacture of Cider and Perry, by T. A. Knight, Esq. F. R. S. and L. S. and President of the Agricultural Society of London.—*London;—Longman and Company.*

"causes,—from a more abundant and regular
"supply of nourishment than is afforded in a state
"of nature, with a favourable climate, or pro-
"tection from the bad effects of an unfavourable
"one. The offspring of every plant and animal,
"when unchanged by cultivation, bears a very
"close resemblance to its parents; but amongst
"the cultivated kind of each, it is extremely va-
"rious; still, however, generally shewing some
"similarity to them. By taking advantage of in-
"cidental variations, and by propagating from
"those individuals which approach nearest to our
"ideas of perfection, improved varieties of fruit,
"as well as of animals, are obtained. Much at-
"tention has, in the present day, been paid to the
"improvement of the latter, whilst the former
"have been almost entirely neglected."   *   *   *
"(p. p. 3, 4, 5th edit).

"The existence of every variety of this fruit
"(the apple), seems to be confined to a cer-
"tain period, during the earlier parts of which,
"only, it can be propagated with advantage to
"the planter. No kind of apple now cultivated,
"appears to have existed more than two hundred
"years; and this term does not at all exceed the
"duration of a healthy tree, or of an orchard, when
"grafted on crab stocks, and planted in a strong
"tenacious soil.   *   *   *

"In the propagation of animals, we can ob
"tain a succession of offspring produced only
"according to the usual course of nature; be
"cause, an animal forms a whole, whose parts
"cannot retain life, when separated from each
"other. The less complex, and less elaborate
"organization of vegetables, admits of other modes
"of propagation; and a detached part of each
"individual, is capable of forming a plant in every
"respect similar to that from which it was taken,
"and possessed of all its powers and properties.
"Vegetable, however, like animal life, in indivi
"duals, appears to have its limits fixed by nature,
"and immortality has alike been denied to the
"oak, and to the mushroom; to the being of a few
"days, and of as many centuries. The general
"law of nature must be obeyed, and each must
"yield its place to a successor. The art of the
"planter readily divides a single tree into almost
"any number that he wishes, but the character of
"the new trees, thus raised, is very essentially
"different from that of a young seedling plant;
"they possess a preternatural maturity, and re
"tain the habits and diseases of the tree, of which
"they naturally formed a part. All efforts which
"have hitherto been made to propagate healthy
"trees, of those varieties which have been long in
"cultivation, have, I believe, been entirely unsuc

"cessful. The grafts grow well for two or three "years, after which, they become cankered and "mossy, and appear, what I consider them really "to be, parts of the bearing branches of old dis- "eased trees." (p. p. 6, 7, and 8).

I shall not follow Mr. Knight into the details of his experiments, which appear to have been most ingenious and minute in their application, and most satisfactory, when viewed in connection with the theory he has established upon them, "that all "plants of this species, however propagated from "the same stock, partake in some degree of the "same life, and will attend the progress of that "life in the habits of its youth, its maturity, and "its decay; though they will not be any way "affected by any incidental injuries the parent "tree may sustain after they are detached from it. "The roots, however, and the trunk adjoining "them, appear to possess, in all trees, a greater de- "gree of durability than the bearing branches "when the old have been destroyed by accident, "or even by old age.

Should the affinity between the apple and the vine, not be considered sufficiently close, to warrant the application to the one species, of the principle established respecting the other, the fact may go far to obviate the objection,— that, from observations made on the fructification of a pea,

Mr. Knight drew conclusions, which enabled him to obtain his most valuable varieties of apples raised from seed. And, when we come to treat of the management of the vine, as prescribed by the French writers, particularly as relates to pruning, and the diseases incident to it; the inference will, I think, appear a most reasonable one, that the French have been long struggling against the effects of age, in most of their varieties: and that to the decay, or extinction of a valuable variety of grape, may probably, with more truth, be imputed the lost, or departing fame, of many vineyards celebrated of old, while others have acquired, or preserved a merited reputation, than to what it is by the French writers generally referred, "the "practice of a blind routine, and the ignorance or "forgetfulness of the laws of nature."

There are authentic records to prove the extraordinary age to which vines will attain; and in ancient, as well as modern history, instances are given of vines, which, for their stature and longevity, were the astonishment of the world: but Lord Bacon long ago remarked, that the lives of trees are greatly prolonged, when their branches are taken off, which could not be the case with those: and Mr. Knight, in the course of his experience, has had occasion to infer, that "in the "culture of the apple and the pear, the life of each

"original tree might be prolonged to three times
"its natural period, by robbing it of its branches
"as soon as the qualities of its fruits were known,
"and retaining it as a pollard, or more properly
"in the state of shoots in a coppice which is felled
"at regular periods; for these are known to possess
"a much greater degree of durability, than the
"same kind of trees, when left in the natural state,
"and to produce a vigorous succession of branches
"during many centuries."

It will be seen, in the passages of the work already alluded to, that some of the operations, recommended to renew vines, bear no very distant resemblance to what is here described; and when it becomes necessary, after 25 or 30 years, (to which period only, the life of vines in some districts extends), to renew a plant which, without such aid, is capable of attaining the age of 600 years, there is little presumption in supposing, that they are the progeny of a parent which was produced in a very remote age; and still less, in deducing the inference already stated, that the French had been led altogether to overlook their propagation by seed.

If, then, from the fickle and fugacious characters of the vine, there is a risk that a valuable variety may lose its desirable properties, when transplanted to a new climate, the gratification of forded by success in the experiment, is still liable to be checked by the fear, that that variety is bordering on decay and dissolution, and may only survive for a few years, to reward the enterprise and industry of its introducer.

Superadded to these considerations, there is this, that out of a considerable number of varieties already introduced, only two have been found effectually to bear the climate of New South Wales.

The plants, indeed, grow luxuriantly, and produce fruit in abundance; but, before arriving at maturity it is very generally attacked by disease or blight. It would seem, that notwithstanding the astonishing facility with which the vine changes its qualities, when in transplantation, it experiences the effects of a slight change of climate or soil, there are changes so violent, that few of its varieties possess the power of altering their habits sufficiently to endure them. It is a curious fact, that in attempting to introduce into America the vines of Europe, obstacles of the same nature should have presented themselves. I have been favoured with the perusal of a memoir made to John M'Arthur, Esq. by a native of Switzerland, who had been engaged in such an undertaking, from which it appears, that his efforts were uniformly disappointed by the effects of blight on the fruit of every variety, with the exception of one, so indifferent in its quality, as almost to have escaped his notice; but from which alone, he was at length, after the repeated failures of the others, reduced to hope for any degree of success.

The varieties, to which those who have experienced the failure of the others in New South Wales, are now confining their attention, are supposed to be the Miller's Burgundy (the meunier of the French) and the claret grape, and another nearly similar to it, which some suppose to be the same, and others to be the ramonat, the grape which produces port wine. To have acquired and naturalized these to the climate of New South Wales, is an important point gained, and reflects honour upon those gentlemen to whom the colony is indebted for them; but several years of experience are still wanting, to ascertain to what extent they retain their valuable properties; and though these, in their highest degree, should be preserved, it should still only act as a stimulus to add to their number, by the introduction of a greater number of varieties. It might also be worth while to ascertain how far a different treatment might avail, in preserving from blight those varieties subject to it. It is common, for instance, in Madeira, to train the vines over a horizontal trellis, and to shade the branches beneath, by the foliage which the trellis supports. That this treatment might prove effectual, may with great probability be inferred, from the complete preservation of those bunches of the blighting varieties, which are enclosed, and allowed to swell and ripen, in paper bags. It is certain, that in the present state of our knowledge on the subject, no experiment is unimportant, from which there is the most distant prospect of deriving useful results. But all the facts we are acquainted with, seem to me to point out in the strongest manner, the importance of obtaining new varieties from seed, and I shall, therefore, quote at some length from Mr. Knight, a description of the methods he found most successful in obtaining new varieties of apples from seed, in the hope, that many may be led to apply the same principles to the vine, from the conviction, that at no distant day, the wine of New South Wales may be equal in importance, to the cider of England, with all the improvement it is susceptible of from the labours of this ingenious philosopher.

"When I first began to suspect," (says Mr. Knight, p. 30) "that my endeavours to propagate

"the old fruits would not be successful, I selected
"the seeds of some of the best kinds, with an in-
"tention to propagate new ones; but I soon found
"that many of the young plants, (particularly
"those of the golden pippin), were nearly as much
"diseased as the trees which produced them. I
"several times raised three or four plants, from
"seeds taken from one apple, and when this had
"been produced by a diseased tree, I have had
"not only as many distinct varieties as there
"were seeds; but some were much diseased, and
"others apparently healthy, though the seeds
"were sown in the same soil, and the plants after-
"wards grew within two feet of each other, in the
"same nursery. Grafts having been inserted from
"each, retained the habits of the tree from which
"they were taken.

"Few, however, if any of them, appeared to
"possess a sufficient degree of vigour to promise
"me much success in their cultivation, (except in
"very favourable situations), should their fruit be
"such as answered my wishes.

"Having before observed, that all the old fruits
"were free from disease when trained to a south
"wall, I thought it not improbable that seedling
"plants, raised from them, would be equally
"healthy; and that this would not be the sole

"advantage attending this mode of propagation,
" as the trees in this situation would enjoy all the
" benefits of a better climate, whilst their blossoms
" being expanded before those of the neighbouring
" orchards, would escape all chance of being im-
" pregnated by the farina of inferior kinds. With
" a view to try the effects of this experiment, I
" prepared stocks of the best kind of apple I
" knew, which could be propagated by cutting,
" and after planting them against a south wall in
" extremely rich mould, I grafted them with the
" stire golden pippin, and a few other fruits, whose
" time of ripening suited the situation in which I
" wished to plant.

" In the course of the ensuing winter, the young
" trees were dug up, and (their roots having been
" retrenched), were again planted in the same
" places. This mode of treatment had the desired
" effect of making some of them produce blossoms
" at two years old.

" I suffered only one or two fruits to remain
" on each tree, which, in consequence, attained
" nearly three times their common size, with a
" very high degree of maturity and perfection;
" and the appearance of the plants I raised from
" their seeds, so much excelled any I had formerly
" obtained from the same fruits taken from the
" orchard, that, I think, I can confidently recom-

" mend the method I have adopted. I had
" chosen fruits possessing excellencies and defects
" of opposite kinds, with a wish to see either
" through the industry of the bees, or my own,
" the effects of a process similar to what is
" called, by breeders of animals, crossing the
" breed. This consists in propagating from males
" and females not related to each other, and is
" certainly necessary, in those animals at least,
" in which strength and spirit constitute excellen-
" cies, to prevent their degenerating. The experi-
" ment was easily made, and the singular effects
" I had seen produced by similar means on other
" plants, left me no reason to doubt that some
" effect would be produced in this. The good
" and the ill effects, which follow the process of
" crossing the breed of plants, are perfectly similar
" to those which have been observed among ani-
" mals. If the male and female be taken from
" two permanent varieties of different characters,
" the immediate offspring will present a mixture
" of both characters in nearly an equal proportion,
" but the progeny of this offspring will be ex-
" tremely various. Some will take nearly the
" form of their male, and others of their female
" ancestry, and it will be long before a new per-
" manent character is acquired. In perennial
" vegetables, the progress of variation and de-

"generacy may be arrested, when an individual
"answering our wishes has been obtained; as this
"individual, by the art of the planter and grafter,
"may be divided and multiplied to almost any
"extent. My experience induces me to believe,
"that the effects of crossing, tend strongly to sti-
"mulate the growth of the offspring, both of plants
"and animals; but that, amongst animals, crosses
"should be made only between breeds bearing a
"good deal of resemblance to each other, or be-
"tween different families of the same breed.

"From the open structure of the blossoms of
"vegetables, and from the numerous tribes of in-
"sects which feed on their honey, or farina, a sexual
"intercourse must, of necessity, take place be-
"tween neighbouring plants of the same species;
"and I am much more disposed to attribute this
"intercourse to the intention, than to the negli-
"gence of nature.

"My wishes were, of course, to correct the
"defects, and to combine the excellencies of the
"best fruits; and I was not without hopes, that
"the offspring would possess a greater degree of
"strength and vigour, as it is known to do in cul-
"tivated animals. A few days, therefore, before
"the blossoms expanded, of the kinds from which
"I wished to propagate, I opened the petals, and
"destroyed the males in all the blossoms, which I

"suffered to remain of one kind, taking great care
"to leave the females uninjured; and when these
"blossoms were fully expanded, I impregnated
"half of them with farina taken from another kind
"of fruit, leaving the other half to the care of the
"bees, which were collected in great numbers,
"owing to the scarcity of flowers at that season,
"and passed busily from one blossom to another.
"I had soon the satisfaction to observe, that every
"fruit which I had impregnated, grew rapidly,
"whilst half of those on the other tree, which had
"remained in their natural state, failed, with
"every one of those left to the care of the bees;
"whence I was disposed to conclude, that these
"insects were not so good carriers of the farina of
"plants, as is, I believe, generally supposed by
"naturalists; but in subsequent experiments,
"where the blossoms of the neighbouring trees
"have been more numerous, I have had reason to
"draw a different conclusion.

"The plants I have obtained from the fruits, on
"which this experiment has been made, are cer-
"tainly much the most promising I have yet seen:
"Some of these possess the character of the male
"parent, others that of the female; in some, that
"of both appears to be blended, and in others, I
"do not distinguish that of either. Many of
"them appear to be perfectly free from hereditary

" disease and debility, and the fruit of some of
" them is not in any degree inferior to those from
" which it derived its existence. Every seed,
" though several were taken from the same apple,
" has afforded a new and distinct variety; and
" some of these grow with more luxuriance than
" others; and the fruits produced by the different
" plants, possess very different degrees of merit.
" An estimate may, in some measure, be made of
" their good and bad qualities, at the conclusion
" of the first summer, by the resemblance the
" leaves bear to the highly cultivated, or wild
" kinds, as has been remarked by the writers on
" this subject, of the 17th century."

It thus appears, that the state of the plant from which the seed is taken, has the strongest influence in forming the character of the seedling plant produced from it, and that it is of the utmost importance, that, when plants are to be propagated by seed, the parent should be in the healthiest state, and the fruit in the highest degree of perfection. Another principle should also be borne in mind, viz. that " the planter must seek those qualities in the parent tree, which he wishes to find in the future seedling plants;" and on reading the following passage, it will readily occur, that the most valuable qualities of a grape, unfit to bear the climate, may, by crossing, be united with that quality, in a variety which perhaps possesses few others to recommend it. "The most effective "method," says Mr. Knight, p. 42, " I have been "able to discover, of obtaining such fruits as "vegetate very early in the Spring, has been by "introducing the farina of the Siberian crab," (a plant which still retains, in England, the habit which it possessed in its native clime, of blossoming on the first appearance of spring), "into the "blossom of a rich and early apple, and by "transferring, in the same manner, the farina of "the apple to the blossom of the Siberian crab. "The leaf and habits of many of the plants I "have thus obtained, possess much the character "of the apple, whilst they vegetate as early in "the spring as the crab of Siberia, and possess, "at least, an equal power of bearing cold; and "I possess two plants of this family, which are "quite as hardy as the most austere crab of our "woods; and are, I think, capable of affording "ciders of much greater merit than any which "have yet existed."

In the large quotations, which I have thus taken the liberty of making from Mr. Knight, the process he recommends, as well as the principles on which it is founded, are so perspicuously described, that it would be presumption in me to attempt adding any thing in explanation; but, as many may be desirous of making the experiments*, who are altogether ignorant of botany, it may not be amiss to observe, that each of the small flowers, or blossoms of the vine, contains five stamina, or male parts of the plant, and one pistil, or female part. These are so called, because their conjunction is, in most cases, necessary for the formation, and in all cases, for the perfection of the fruit. The male parts are small awl-shaped filaments, surrounding the female, which they rise above, and spreading a little outwards; their extremities, called antheræ, are covered with the pollen or farina. From the smallness of the flowers of the vine, the operation will, of course, be more difficult and nice than in the apple; but every thing will yield to care and perseverance.

---

* I have observed, that at the last meeting of the Agricultural Society of New South Wales, some dissatisfaction was manifested, on the part of some of the members, at the manner in which the premiums were distributed. I hope it will not be taken ill, if one who is as yet a stranger to their body, though not to all its members, should suggest the application of some of the funds, intended for premiums, to the advancement of the object here recommended.

Such stimuli would appear to be afforded with peculiar propriety, to objects which, though most beneficial to the public, and likely, eventually, to be so in a very high degree to the individual, are yet new, and of more distant and less obvious advantage.

Speechly, who has very strenuously recommended the attempt to raise new varieties of vines by seed, and who seems to have had a very clear idea of the advantage which Mr. Knight's experiments have since ascertained to be obtainable by a mixture of varieties, affirms, that by judicious management, seedling vines will bear fruit the third or fourth year. There will, therefore, be no great loss of time in ascertaining the qualities of their fruit. The management he prescribes, is exactly the same as that for a cutting.

As soon as the wood of the seedling plant is ripe, though the quality of the fruit is not ascertained, it will be advantageous to plant a few cuttings from it; that, if it should turn out a valuable variety, a greater quantity of plants may be the sooner obtained.

It is, however, one of the strongest facts which support Mr. Knight's theory, that he has found it impossible to anticipate the natural period of a seedling, apples bearing, by grafting a cutting from it on a bearing tree; and it is, therefore, most probable, that it would be equally unsuccessful with the vine.

The length at which I have treated this part of the subject, has swelled the chapter to a size disproportionate to the other divisions of the work, but not to the opinion I have of its importance. It is, in fact, the foundation on which a successful cultivation of the vine, in New South Wales, must be raised; and a point which, if attended to in time, may save the expenditure of immense sums in a nugatory manner, and determine, not only the degree of success which may attend the cultivation of the vine, but in a great measure the expense at which that success must be purchased.

The following notice of the principal varieties of vines cultivated in France, is preceded by a table of the characters by which they are described. These are drawn from the leaves and fruit, as being less liable to change than some others, such as the distance of the knots, the colour of the bark, &c. The leaf is always understood to be perfect, and of the largest size.

Each variety has a different name, in almost every province or district where it is cultivated.

The *maurillon hatif;* or forward maurillon. It is the earliest variety of the climate; its berries take a black colour long before their maturity; they are small, round, and not close; their skin is hard and thick, the pulp dry and fibrous; its juice is almost insipid; the bunches and leaves small; the leaves of a bright green on both surfaces, and terminated by a large and broad indentation. Excepting in Provence, it is not cultivated, having no other merit than precocity.

The *meunier*, or miller, called also mealy maurillon; its leaves are covered with a white cottony matter, whence the name; it seems an improved variety of the preceding; its berries are black, large, and rather close in the bunch, which is short and thick; its leaves are three lobed, having, besides, two divisions which, if a little deeper, would form two semilobes.

The white *savaguien*, only differs from the preceding in the colour of the fruit, and the greater size of the bunch; the grapes are also larger, and more oblong; the two lower lobes of the leaf, have also a more decided character.

The *maurillon*, or *pineau* of Burgundy. It is more than probable that it takes it name from its black colour, or colour of the moor; because many black grapes, of a different kind, are also called maurillon; the best vineyards of Burgundy

The most characteristic Marks for dist¹.

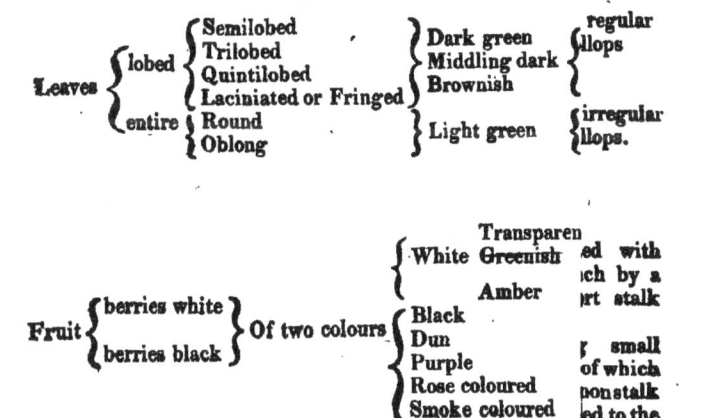

Leaves { lobed { Semilobed / Trilobed / Quintilobed / Laciniated or Fringed } { Dark green / Middling dark / Brownish } { regular llops / irregular llops. }
entire { Round / Oblong } { Light green }

Fruit { berries white / berries black } Of two colours { White { Transparen / Greenish / Amber } / Black / Dun / Purple / Rose coloured / Smoke coloured } ed with ch by a rt stalk small of which on stalk ed to the

are chiefly composed of this grape; the bunch is only of a middling size, and the grapes not large nor close on the bunch; the bark is reddish, the leaf lightly divided into five lobes, and very regularly indented round the edges; it does not announce much vigour of vegetation.

The white *morillon* has a longer branch than the preceding; the berries are almost round, and compose a bunch of little clusters; the leaf, without being entire, is not lobed, but is very distinctly indented round the edge; its upper surface is green, and its under whitish; it is supported by a large and red petiole.

The *franc pineau*, the *morillon* par excellence. The bunch is short and rather conic; the berry oblong, and close to the bunch—of a carnation red at the orifice; the wool is slender, long, and inclined to red; the knots distant from each other, and when the wood is cut transversely, a reddish colour is observeable in it; the petiole of the leaf is long, the leaf short, red, and semilobed on two sides—delicately indented round the edge; its colour is rather a deep green on the upper, and pale on the under surface, and both surfaces covered with down; it produces little, but the taste of its fruit is excellent, and the most delicate wines of Burgundy are made from it.

The black Burgundy, *(Borguignon noir)*. This

variety is also one of the black morillons; by the form of its berry, it has some analogy with the preceding, but it is less oblong in proportion to its size, and much less close to the bunch, the stalks of which are red; the wood inclines to brown, and is closely knotted; the leaf is obtuse towards the point, and slightly divided into five parts, regularly indented; its petiole is short, and very red; the bunch has a winged form, is shouldered.

The white *grivet*. The bunch is short, unequally formed, and of a middling size; the berries round, rather close, and of a sweet perfumed taste; its colour is greyish, and it is thought to be a variety of the *franc pineau*; it is not now so much cultivated as formerly.

The *sauvignon*. This, as well as the preceding, was much more cultivated formerly; its strong perfume gave a peculiar character to the wine made from it, but producing little, its plantation has been discontinued; its bunch is short, rather small than large, of a whitish colour, inclining to yellow, and of an amber colour where exposed to the sun; towards its maturity, it is covered with small brick red spots, which are characteristic of it; its leaf is not lobed, but very deeply and regularly indented, and forms three large scollops towards its top.

Black and white *Rochelle.* It is very common in the north east of France, but is not in request among those who prefer quality to quantity of produce; its leaf is divided into five lobes, the upper more large than the inferior; the border is deeply indented; it has a long footstalk; it is of a fine green on the upper surface, and whitish and cottony beneath; it is remarkable for the elegance of its form.

The *teinturier*, or dyer. This variety possesses characteristic marks, not only in the form of its fruit and leaves, but in the very deep red colour of its expressed juice, and the almost carnation colour which its leaves assume, long before the maturity of the fruit; its bunch is unequal, and winged; it is terminated by an imperfect cone; its berries are round and unequal; its leaf is deeply indented, and divided into five lobes; it has something rustic in its appearance. It is only cultivated for colouring wines; fermented separately, it affords a harsh and ill-tasted liquor.

The *ramonat* has some resemblance to the preceding, as to the colour of its juice, but it is a much superior fruit, and yields much better wine; the berries and bunch are larger, and the wood stronger; the leaf wider, and in one variety two lobed, in another four lobed.

The pearl grape. The berry of this variety is

oblong, having a long petiole; the bunch is formed of many little clusters; from its appearance, one would say, that it could, with difficulty, support its weight; it has an elongated appearance; the leaf would be very regularly indented, if, besides the two lobes which divide its upper part, it had not a semilobe on the upper part of the right side.

The *mélier;* or white *meruair.* This grape, whose bunch bears, at first sight, a strong resemblance to the chapelas, frequently goes by its name, though different from it in many respects. The colour which it contracts, on the side exposed to the sun, is rather reddish than yellow; its young leaves have not that beautiful rosy colour for which those of the chapelas are remarkable; its berries are round, plump, and separate, and ripen well even in the north of France; its juice is sweet and agreeable; the leaf is very deeply divided, and has a common petiole, half red, which separates into five reddish glands; it is divided into five very deep lobes, and very much broken in its circumference; of a pale green colour above, whitish below, and covered with a light down.

There is a variety of this, little different in the form and quality of its fruit, but very much so in its leaf; it has two semilobes in its upper part; its lower part is only divided by two cuts, a little deeper than the rest of the indenting.

The green *Rochelle.* The bunch of this variety is of a middling size; the berries have a soft skin, and are close; even at its highest degree of maturity, it has an acid sweetish taste which is not agreeable. It almost always produces with a kind of abundance, and is reputed very advantageous for the manufacture of brandy. The leaf, divided into two principal lobes, besides two semilobes, is very thick; its upper surface is darkish green, its under surface ash coloured, and covered with a very short down; the wood is yellow, and closely knotted; the petiole, red, short, and round, is terminated by five glands, the middle one much larger than the others.

The *Rochelle blonde;* or fair Rochelle, which seems to be a degeneration of the preceding, has only two lobes in the upper part of the leaf; the lower part is entire; the colour of its foliage, as well as of its fruit, is of a much lighter green.

The large *muscadet.* There are two kinds of the muscadet *enfumé,* or *smoked;* the large, and small; the leaf of the first has a large petiole, which parts into five glands; the upper surface is of a dark, and the under of a whitish green, but without down; all its edge is lightly indented, but there is only one deep division on the right side; the stalk of the bunch is not strong; the berry is of an undecided colour, between white and a light rose colour.

The leaves of the little *muscadet* are smaller; they are lobed on their upper part, and the indentation of their border is more acute; it is also called muscadine.

The *round leaf*. The berries of this variety are rather oblong, and so close in the bunch, that, in fertile soils, it is not uncommon to see the least adherent fall to the ground to give place to others; the maturity of the fruit is announced by the yellow colour by which it is gilded; its leaf is large, not lobed, and its petiole is divided into three principal glands; it is of a paler green below than above, and is covered with a very fine down.

The white *gouet;* or *gouais*. The bunch of this variety is large, and composed of larger grapes in general than those of the muscat, to which it would have more resemblance, if the berries were closer on the bunch; the leaf is entire, or unlobed, but is deeply and unequally indented; it is supported by a grey and slender footstalk.

The black *gamé*. This variety almost every where produces abundantly, but its produce is of divers qualities; in certain soils, and under certain latitudes, it concurs happily to the formation of the best wines. In other places it has been extirpated for its bad qualities. Every thing in the gamé announces the richest vegetation; the wood is large, the knots distant, but also large; the leaf thick, of a deep green, not lobed, scolloped in large divisions, and these irregularly indented; the peduncule and petiole large and strong.

The little *gamé* resembles the good morillon in the form of its bunch, and of its berries, but it has neither its taste nor sweetness; it is very black; two semilobes divide its leaf into three parts; the indentation of the upper is more unequal than that of the lower division.

The *mausard*. The bunch of this variety is of a considerable size, and is of a regular pyramidical form. It is not uncommon to see it nine or ten inches in length, and four or five in diameter; the berries are large, and middling close; the wood is strong, and brown or blackish; the leaf large, thick, very green, and lightly indented in proportion to its size.

The *murleau*. This variety announces much vigour, by the strength of its wood, and of its knots; the leaf has nothing extraordinary in its proportions, but it is lobed in its upper part, and very remarkable for the delicacy and inequality of the indentation of its border; the bunch is winged.

or shouldered, and is of a fine velvet black; its berries are rather close towards the base.

The gilded, or golden *chapelas*. The bunch is large, and formed of unequal berries, with a hard skin; when ripe, their colour is yellowish, and the side exposed to the sun takes an amber colour; the leaves are very deeply indented, and the indentations are large and wide; the petiole very long.

A subvariety of the chapelas, is the *blanquette* or *domre;* it is an excellent eating grape, but yields bad wine.

The red *chapelas*, is also a variety of the preceding; the bunch and the berries are smaller; the sides exposed to the sun are tinged with a red colour, but of a clear green on the shady side.

The musked *chapelas*. The berry is round, and almost as large as that of the gilded chapelas, but is not amber on the nunced side; and, in its perfect maturity, it preserves its light green colour; its leaf is also smaller, but of a deeper green; it is deeply indented, and has a long footstalk; the chapelas ripens perfectly, even in the north of France, and the fruit is excellent, but it is no where remarkable for yielding a good wine. The musked is fifteen days later in ripening than the gilded chapelas.

The *ciotat*, or Austrian grape. If this variety were classed by the colour and taste of its fruit, it would be ranked with the chapelas; when under the same exposure, it ripens at the same time; the bunch is smaller, and the berry less round than those of the chapelas; it is remarkable for its palm-like fringed leaves, which are divided into five parts; they have a common petiole, which divides into five parts, and extends to the extremities of the leaf.

Another variety is called also *persillade*, from the resemblance of its leaves to those of parsley (*parsil*); it is also distinguished from the preceding, by the red colour of its fruit.

The white *muscat*. The berries of this variety are large and oblong; they take an amber colour on the side exposed to the sun; the bunches are long and narrow, and terminate in a point, the berries being very close; it is only in the southern districts of France that it attains to maturity; its leaf is of a deeper green than that of the chapelas, and is very distinctly divided into five parts, the indentations of its edges being irregular.

The red *muscat*. This has the merit of ripening more easily than the preceding, because its berries are less close on the bunch; its flower is, however, extremely delicate, and is frequently abortive; it has less perfume than the white muscat; the bunch is elongated, and supported by a very long footstalk; the berries, exposed to the sun, are of a very bright red, approaching to purple; the leaves, which resemble those of the preceding, redden towards autumn.

The violet *muscat*. The leaves of this variety correspond exactly with those of the white muscat; the berries are large, and rather long; their skin is hard, and of a deep violet colour, and covered with a mealy substance. This is the black Constantia of the Cape.

The *muscat* of Alexandria. This variety has a very strong flavour of musk, when ripe, but it scarcely ripens even in the most southern provinces of France; it has little resemblance to the other varieties of the muscat, its leaves being quite free from the deep divisions which distinguish them; the indentation of its border is almost nothing, but the scollops (larger indentations) are very remarkable, and very acute; the berries are large, oblong, and regular, rather more swelled below, than at the insertion of the stalk; without being pressed upon each other, they form very fine bunches; a fine amber colour indicates their perfect maturity.

The grape of *Maror*, or *African grape*. The berries are unequal, of the form of a heart, and of an undecided violet colour; they compose very large bunches; all the plant announces a most vigorous vegetation; the stalks are strong, and the leaves large; they are deeply divided, and surrounded by a deep and acute indentation. In the climate of France, it is destitute of quality.

The *cornichon*. The form of this grape is remarkable; it is crooked, and pointed towards the extremity, whence the name cornichon, (a little horn); it, however, bears more resemblance to a fish's bladder, than to any other object to which it can be compared; it is frequently near two inches in length, and three fourths of an inch in its thickest part, where it bears two seeds, terminated by a point, and nearly as long as the diameter of the berry; the reunion of several small clusters, on long footstalks, forms a bunch of no great volume; the leaf of this variety is large, and almost entire; the indentations of the edge very unequal; the fruit turns yellow when ripe.

The white Corinth grape, called also *pape*, and *paperille;* the bunch is winged, long, and formed of small berries which do not press upon each other; the skin is mealy, and coloured like the chapelas on the side exposed to the sun; the leaf is large and cloth-like; its upper surface is of a light green, and its under surface covered with a cottony matter; it is divided into five parts, but the divisions are not deep; its edge rather cut than indented, presents long and acute points; the Corinth grape is destitute of seeds.

The name of paperille was given by the Greeks, and after them by the Italians and Spaniards, to those kinds, of which they twisted the stalk to allow them to dry upon the stock.

What, in France, is called the Corinth grape, differs very materially from the original Corinth grape, which is cultivated so largely in Zante, for its dried fruits, known in England under the name of Zante currants.

The *verjuice*. It is so called in the northern and central departments of France, because, it never ripens its fruits. It is also called *Bordelais*. The variety most resembling it, in the vicinity of Bordeaux, is called *pumelas* and *chalope*, but it ripens so perfectly, that the berry frequently detaches itself from the bunch, before the vintage. Its berries are oblong, and very large, and compose small clusters, which, by their reunion, make very large bunches; the leaf is large, almost round, and very sensible of the effects of frost; and it is, perhaps, to this extreme delicacy that its little ripeness, in countries where the frosts are early, is to be attributed.

A vine, from a seed of this variety, planted many years ago, in the well known garden of the chevalier Janson, at Chaillot, near Paris, has produced a variety, whose fruit reaches the highest maturity, and is of an excellent quality.

Swiss or *Aleppo grape*. The berry of this variety is streaked; it is liable to degenerate; it is sometimes altogether black, and more frequently white; in autumn its leaves are streaked with red, green, and yellow, in a similar manner to those of the Aleppo lettuce. It is more an object of curiosity, than economy.

CHAPTER THIRD.

Of the Preparation of the Soil, the Choice of Plants, and different Methods of Planting.

WHEN the cultivator, having applied the principles of the first chapter, to the situation in which he finds himself placed, and having combined as many favourable circumstances as may be compatible with it, has fixed upon the site of his vineyard, it becomes his next care, to prepare the soil for the reception of the plants; and for this purpose, that proceeding is best which is most effectual in clearing it from weeds, and reducing it to a friable and porous state.

The depth to which it is necessary to labour the soil, depends upon its nature, and the nature of the climate. In colder climates, a less depth is sufficient, because the plant is not suffered to grow to a large size, and has consequently less need that its roots should penetrate deep. Where a warmer climate allows the enlargement of its dimensions, it is, of course, requisite, that its roots should extend in proportion, and that the soil should be prepared to such a depth, as may not oppose their dissemination.

In some climates it would appear, that no soil could be too dry, or too shallow for the vine; cases being mentioned, as occurring in some districts of France, to which the ordinary means of tillage are quite inapplicable, and where it is necessary, in the first instance, to blast the decomposing rocks, and afterwards, by mallets, to reduce them to the size of nuts, or peas. An instance of this kind is described, where a proprietor, by these means, reduced a naked calcareous rock, and planted upon it the vine, which, to the surprise of every one, not only succeeded, but produced, and, after forty years, continued to produce the finest wine of the district.

As a preparation for the soil intended for wines, it is common in Burgundy to sow lucerne and sainfoin, which have the advantage of destroying parasitical plants, while their long roots serve to reduce the soil to a loose and permeable state. Before the vines are planted, these roots and stalks are carefully collected and burned, and their ashes spread on the soil. Crops of beans, or potatoes, are also recommended, not only on account of the labours they require, but because the manure which it is necessary to give them, is, when its grosser parts are volatilized, beneficial to the young plants.

While the soil is in the course of preparation, the larger stones should be collected, and these may be usefully employed for enclosures; or, if the ground is steep, for forming terraces, to prevent the soil from being carried down by the rain. Where there are no stones to form enclosures, even ditches are recommended, in preference to live hedges, which ought never to be allowed to exceed three feet in height.

The most common methods of propagating vines, are, by cuttings, by rooted plants, and by layers. Of these methods, that by cuttings is most recommended, and most generally practised. A good cutting should consist of a shoot of one year's growth, together with a small piece of the older wood attached to it; not that this adds in any respect to its goodness, but because it shows, that one shoot has not been divided into several cuttings, as those buds nearest the bottom send forth the strongest shoots.

Rooted plants, which are cuttings prepared for two or three years in a nursery or garden, are generally found to languish so much, from the change of soil, and from the injuries the very minute and numerous fibres of the roots have sustained, as well as from the want of that care to which plants in a nursery are accustomed, but which cannot be extended to them on a larger scale, as to make it doubtful whether much advantage is obtained by the process—and whether more time is required by cuttings, for the developement of their roots, or by rooted plants, to reconcile themselves to their new situation.

Rooted plants are also procured by layers. A strong shoot being chosen in spring, and the buds nearest the stock being carefully removed, it is bent carefully into a small trench, prepared for it. The extremity, which rises above, is fixed to a small prop, and in autumn a rooted plant is obtained, when, or at the commencement of spring, it may be separated. A better method is, to carry the shoot through a basket of earth; but this is too expensive to be practised on a large scale.

The greatest caution is recommended, in selecting the stocks, from which to take cuttings. When the mother plant has not finished half its career, it is still endued with all its vegetative energy, therefore, they should have reached the age of eight or ten years, where the vines subsist during twenty-five or thirty years, and from twenty to thirty years, where they endure a hundred. It ought to be ascertained, that they produce large and well ripened fruit; that their wood is strong,

P

sound, and without blemish or bruise. Their qualities should never be left to chance, but after the kinds of vines to be propagated are determined upon, the vineyards should be examined in autumn, just before the vintage, and those which are most healthy and vigorous, marked with a thread, or a twig of osier. From these only, the cuttings should be taken, when the wood is perfectly ripened, which it generally is, after the leaf has fallen. It is necessary that they should be of such a length, that, after having part of their upper extremity cut off, they may be put from nine to fifteen inches into the ground.

If the vineyard is to consist of several varieties, care must be taken to place each in the most favourable circumstances.

First, there should be one grand division of white and coloured varieties; the coloured varieties generally ripen ten or twelve days earlier than the white; they should, therefore, be planted in the lowest part of the vineyard. The great object is, to have every variety ripe at the same time, and, therefore, those varieties which differ considerably in the period of their maturity, should not be planted together; and as far as situation will effect it, the others should be so placed, that the forward may be restrained, and the tardy accelerated. Those which ripen with the greatest difficulty, always shew vigour of vegetation, they should, therefore, be planted in the least fertile part of the soil; and the bottom part of the slope, or the richest part, should be appropriated to those which are more valuable for the quality, than the quantity of their produce.

It will thus be necessary, that the cuttings of each variety should be tied up separately, and marked.

The time of planting is different, in different climates. In the warmer climates, if this operation is deferred till spring, it frequently happens, that the young plant has not time to acquire strength to resist the heats of summer, while the temperature of the atmosphere, besides, seldom falls so low, as altogether to stop vegetation; and there is generally established, at the extremity of the plant, a sort of movement, which, if it does not give birth to apparent roots, so disposes the plant, nevertheless, to produce them, that they burst forth spontaneously in the first of the fine weather.

In colder climates, it is otherwise, and to plant before the winter, would be to risk the success of the plantation. The humidity of the soil would tend to rot that part of the plant below the surface; and the two eyes left above, would frequently be so much injured, as to be incapable of developing their buds.

Where, then, the winters are severe and wet, the plantation must be deferred to the spring, and there is, in this case, also less danger from the more moderate heat of the summer. But where the winters are mild, the planting in autumn affords many advantages

When it is necessary to preserve the cuttings, some time before they are planted, they should be tied in bundles, and kept in a cellar, buried in damp sand, with two or three of the eyes of the upper extremities exposed to the air. In some places they are preserved in trenches, opened in a dry soil; and, if care is taken that they should not press too much on one another, they will be found, when drawn out for plantation, to have put forth, from the lowest eyes, numerous small roots. It is rare that a plant, in this state, if properly managed, does not succeed.

The distance at which the plants are placed, is determined by the height to which it is intended they should be confined, and this again depends upon the climate. In the colder climates, they are frequently planted so close, as from one and a half to two feet, and it is conceived that this closeness serves to protect them from frosts, and assists their ripening, by increasing the temperature of the air, in consequence of its circulating less.

In proportion as the heat of the climate is more

capable of elaborating the juices of a larger plant, they are placed at a greater distance, and this distance sometimes extends to six feet. For vines of a middling height, three feet in the rows, and from three, to three and a half feet a-part, are the most common distances, unless it is intended, as is frequently the case in the south of France, to sow corn in the intervals, in which case they are to be seen at all distances.

The method of planting usually adopted for cuttings, where the soil has sufficient consistency, is the dibble. It is made something in the form of a large auger, or like the letter T, the cross bar being wood, and has an iron projection, or stop, about the depth to which the plant is intended to enter. The depth varies according to the distance, it being necessary to preserve a proportion between the roots and the branches. Where they are to be very close, from seven to nine inches in depth will be sufficient; and where they are to be of larger growth, and more distant, from twelve to fifteen inches.

Whatever be the depth determined upon, the plant must be cut down, to leave only two knots, or eyes, above the surface. It is always the knot nearest the surface, which parts the stock; and if any thing occurs to destroy it, or prevent its shooting, it is only necessary to uncover, with the finger, the next lower eye, which will immediately supply its place. Before planting, the cutting is kept in water from the time of its being cut; if new, or from the time of its being taken from the trench or cellar, where it has been preserved; after being introduced into the hole, a few handfuls of fine mould, or what is more common, of wood ashes, are put about it, and some pour in water, or the drainage of dunghills. If the ground slopes, the plant should be placed a little opposed to its inclination. Where the slope of the ground is gentle, it is recommended to open trenches, from one end to the other, giving them a depth proportioned to the distance of the plants. This is the best method, especially for rooted plants; a quantity of fine mould is also generally spread where the plant is to be placed. If it is a rooted plant, it will require all the care which is usually given to young trees, none of which are more susceptible of injury.

It is of great importance, as facilitating the various labours they receive, that the plants should have a regular arrangement, that of a quincunx is recommended, and possesses, in this respect, great advantages; but it often happens, that the irregularity of the ground, and the stony soil, will not allow of this, in which case, it is necessary to dig a hole, if the dibble cannot be used, whenever opportunity offers, care being taken to place the uppermost and finest soil at the bottom of the hole, and nearest to the plant.

It is a very common practice, to place two plants in the row, inclining one to the right, and the other to the left; but this is very much disapproved of, as forcing the roots to intermingle, and stifle each other.

It is particularly recommended, to finish planting in one season, and to preserve a few cuttings, or plants, to replace any which may not have taken; and, finally, to finish, by making the soil perfectly level and smooth.

CHAPTER FOURTH.

Of the height of Vines, and of their Pruning and Supports.

FROM the dwarf vine, pruned to within a few inches of the ground, to that which overtops the elm which it clings to for support, there is every variety in the height of vines.

Those which are supported by trees, are common in Italy and Spain, and are occasionally met with in some of the most southern districts of France. Some are supported by poles, to various heights; and others are allowed to trail their branches on the ground, or to support them as their strength or direction will allow.

The highest kinds of vines, not supported by trees, are frequently trained on poles, joined in a sort of trellis, to the height of from seven to ten feet. The stocks of others, are kept from two and a half to four and a half feet in height, and supported by poles of the height of six feet.

In situations, exposed to high winds or storms, three of these poles are frequently joined together at top, forming a triangle, to which the shoots of various stocks are attached, and are thus mutually supported, and the grapes preserved from being bruised or destroyed. This method of culture is very common, from the shores of the Mediterranean, to the neighbourhood of Lyons, and is the method practised at Cotie Rotie, and Condrieu, where it is directed with much care.

In general, as we approach a colder climate, we see the vines reduced in their dimensions.

The proportion which it is necessary to preserve between the sap circulating in the plant, and the heat which is to modify that sap, will not admit of a larger growth; besides, it is only near the surface of the earth that there is a sufficient degree of heat to ripen the grapes. In warmer climates, a vine is capable of bringing to maturity a large portion of fruit, and its height, and its branches, may be proportionably increased; but there seems, in this respect, a bound which may not be passed with advantage. It is not only because the fruit of those vines, supported by trees, is, by their foliage, shaded from the rays of the sun, that they yield wine of an inferior description. It is the nature of the vine, to absorb moisture by its leaves, in much greater proportion than by its roots; and this unmeasured foliage continues to supply a quantity of sap, which circulates without elaboration, and is rather employed in the formation of wood, and the grapes, consequently, contain an aqueous fluid, which it is impossible to convert into a wine of good quality.

Trees which are pruned, never attain the size and strength of those, the branches of which grow old with them, because, by pruning off so much of the wood, a larger proportion of the sap is forced into the fruit, than would naturally flow to it. Qualities are thus produced in fruits, which, naturally, they would not attain; and there are two sorts of maturity, that which nature, left to herself, gives, which is sufficient to propagate, by seed, the plant in its natural climate, and that which art procures, in carrying the fruit to a higher degree of perfection, at the expense of the other parts of the tree. In the vine, there may be said to be a third sort of maturity; that which gives, in a high degree, the principles on which depend the qualities of the wine made from its fruits; for these are often masked by a taste which is unpleasant to the palate, and are frequently wanting when the palate is most flattered by the fruit.

Thus, the grape may be brought to a tolerable degree of perfection, as a fruit, in a much colder climate than it would naturally grow, and in a climate where, naturally, it would be a slender shrub, bearing sour grapes; it may be brought to yield fruit, possessing, in a high degree, the vinous principles; but it does not appear, that, in the climates most favourable for it, and where its dimensions are greatest, it ever naturally brings its fruits to that state of maturity, in which they would undergo the vinous fermentation. For the attainment of this object, it is necessary, in all cases, to reduce the size of the plants, and concentrate that sap, which would tend to the production and enlargement of the wood, to the perfecting of the fruit. This end cannot be obtained, even in the warmest climates of France, in a plant of greater height than four and a half feet, including the mother branches; and perhaps no cultivator, who is not regardless of the quality of his wine, should allow it to exceed this height. But even in countries, enjoying every advantage of climate, and vineyards, possessing the most suitable soil and situation, the cultivator sometimes finds it his interest, to confine its growth to the dimensions more common in less favourable climates. Thus, in the best vineyards of Medóc, producing the claret wines, the vines do not exceed eighteen inches, or two feet, in height. The best vines of Sicily, (those of Mr. Wodehouse), are also of a dwarf size, and are confined to the production of four bunches each.

If the cuttings, which form a new plantation,

have been well selected, and the operation of planting, conducted with care, they will have sent out, at the end of the first year, a shoot from each of the eyes left above the surface; and, if the wood is sufficiently ripe, these must be pruned; but, if they have not attained sufficient consistence, the pruning must be deferred till the following year. The object of pruning, in this case, is to concentrate the juices of the plants, which would run to the formation of crowds of useless shoots and leaves, to the strengthening or forming of one stock, or stem. In the first pruning, the shoot from the uppermost knot, or eye, should be entirely removed, and the other cut above the first eye. In the second year, if it be destined for a vine of from four to five feet in height, it should be pruned above three shoots, and the others removed close to the stock; for a lower vine, two shoots are sufficient; and for a dwarf vine, one, and this should be the lowest. In all cases, only the lowest eye should be left to each shoot.

In the third year, an additional eye may be left on each of the mother branches, which still ought to be confined to three, and should rarely exceed four, even in its most advanced state. Two mother branches are sufficient for the lower vine; that is, one which is allowed to grow from two and a half to three and a half feet in height; and it is only from the trunk, or stock, of the dwarf vine, that the fruit-bearing branches should issue, those which are lowest being always preferred, if their inclination is not such, as to expose the fruit to the contact of the ground.

At the fourth year, a well planted vine has acquired strength to give fruit—two eyes may be left on two or three of the strongest shoots. The pruning in the fifth season, still requires particular management; two eyes should be left only on the strongest of the new wood, and that which has less vigour, should retain only one; the whole number of the branches of young wood thus left, should not exceed five. The young plant has now become a *made* vine.

The care of the cultivator, must not, however, be relaxed;—the same principles which have hitherto directed him, should guide him in future;—but the plant, having acquired more vigour, will require more minute attention in the pruning.

There are circumstances by which he must be guided, in leaving a greater quantity of bearing branches, or retrenching their number: these are, the nature of the climate, the exposure, the nature of the soil, the vigour of the plant, the quality of the wood formed the preceding year. The age of the vine ought, also, to be considered, and the kind to which it belongs; one kind, is famous for ripening a large quantity of grapes; another, is capable of bringing only a small quantity of grapes to perfection. The vine, too heavily charged, is soon exhausted; too lightly, it yields little but wood.

In the warmer climates of the south of France, a vine of four and a half or five feet in height, and proportionally distant from other plants, may support, on each of its three or four mother branches, five or six young branches; and on each of these, from four to six eyes may be left without inconvenience. The lower vines, which are more closely planted, and have only two mother branches, are sufficiently charged with two or three shoots on each; and on these, two or three eyes may be left according to the strength of the wood.

The dwarf vine is not forked, and the plants are still closer; three or four shoots are sufficient to leave on it, and one or two eyes, on each of these, will charge it in proportion to its strength.

The necessity of adhering to a system of pruning, which will equalize, as much as possible, the fruit which a vine is allowed to bear to its strength, is so great, that there are few instances of vines being let. The interest of the farmer, might induce him to leave a quantity of fruit on the vine, which would destroy its future capacity for bearing.

Thus, to charge a plant as heavily as it will bear, and to charge it to death, are synonimous expressions.

An old vine requires the same care and attention, as when it was still in its infancy; it requires to be pruned close, and the old wood frequently renewed; this makes shoots, which spring from the bottom of the stick, of great value, although at first sterile. Not only age, but the numerous accidents to which the vine is subject, make this measure necessary. When a vine is so much injured by frost, that an after budding cannot be reckoned on, the old and new wood is cut close to the stock. A vine should also be pruned above, when its yellow and sickly appearance indicates that worms have attacked its roots. If, on the contrary, in the year preceding, the abortion of the flower has disappointed the hopes of fruit, and the sap has been employed in forming shoots of unmeasured length, there is nothing risked in leaving a larger quantity of bearing wood, and charging it amply with fruit; as, if a little exhausted, it can be pruned proportionally shorter in the following year. In dry seasons, the vine makes little wood, and should be pruned short, as also, if the winter has been severe. If the wood and the fruit buds have been in part frozen, they should not be hastily removed; there is still room to expect a harvest from the after buds. When the weather has become mild, the branches which have suffered, may be removed above the uninjured buds.

In the operation of pruning, care should be taken, that the instrument of the workman be sharp, that the wood may not be bruised. The cut should be an inch from the nearest eye, and sloping from the side opposite to it.

A question which divides agriculturists, is, whether it is more advantageous to prune in autumn, or in spring; and this is a question which each cultivator must determine for himself, by the nature of the climate under which his vines are situated. It is rather a question to be determined by circumstances, than by a general rule. If, on the one hand, the vine is pruned in autumn, the wood may be still unripe; and it is an observation, whose truth has been confirmed by long experience, that a vine, pruned before the wood has reached maturity, is sure to perish in the course of three or four years. If the operation is delayed till the complete maturity of the wood, it has much to fear from the severity of the winter, as, from its open and spongy nature, it is very susceptible of injury from frosts and moisture.

If, on the other hand, the operation is delayed till spring, the frosts so frequently encroach upon the time of vegetation, that in shunning danger from these, the sap commences to circulate, and weeps from the wounds, to the great impoverishment of the plant. The autumn pruning, too, hastens the shooting of the wood the following year, and in late kinds, brings the fruit to an earlier maturity; and, as the interest of the cultivator is, to have all his kinds ripe at the same period, this may be so managed, as to be subservient in procuring a simultaneous ripeness among the varieties. It is, however, the most common practice, to defer the operation till spring; and, in all cases, it is most important, that the weather should be settled, and fine.

Various supports are used for vines, as their height may require, as the value of their produce may make every thing important, which can contribute in any way to their improvement. In many places, where the ground is dry, supports are altogether dispensed with for low vines, though nature, by giving tendrils to the upper part of its branches, seems to indicate the dependence of the plant, on a foreign support. It is strongly recommended, to train the vines on a trellis; but in wine countries, in general, the wood is so expensive, that a trellis is seldom seen supporting any but vines of the highest stature, not supported by trees. The common practice, is to fix a pole between two plants, to which the branches are fastened, by twigs of osier; and too little care is generally bestowed, in giving a proper direction to the branches.

The natural course of the sap is vertical; and when this is assisted by the direction of the branches, it rushes with astonishing force to the extremities of the young shoots, where it is wasted in the production of new and useless wood; when, on the contrary, the branches are fixed horizontally, or even in a semicircular position, its natural course is interrupted and it is the better elaborated, as it circulates with less vehemence.

The direction in which the trellis extends, is not a matter of indifference. Where the vines are subject to be injured by frost, their arrangement to face the east, would only expose them to the greater danger from the rising sun. But, when exposed to the south, the frost has already yielded to the heat of the atmosphere, before they receive his direct rays. In hotter countries, again, it would appear necessary, rather to protect the fruit from the burning influence of the sun's rays, as at Madeira, where the vines are trained over a low horizontal lattice work, under which, the fruit ripens in the shade.

The vines being thus pruned, and attached to their supports, the first of the fine weather has

has scarcely appeared, when the buds have already begun to burst forth. But the labour of the cultivator has not yet terminated. Three distinct operations are described, by which the branches are successively stopt in their growth, relieved from their useless shoots, and in part, from their leaves. But these are operations which ought not, in all circumstances, to take place; they depend not only on the nature of the climate, but on the state of the weather. Thus, in a climate rather mild than warm, as in a great part of France, the vine-dresser sees the unmeasured length of the shoots, and fears that all the sap will be converted into wood, and that the fruit will be deprived of the share necessary to its maturity. To cause the reflux of the sap towards the grape, he cuts off the extremity of the shoot; this has the wished for effect, but it also escapes in numerous small shoots through the lower eyes, and these are, from the same principle, in the same manner, lopped off. When these operations are performed in a colder climate, or a wet season, they are attended with excellent effects, though not in the manner which the operator generally conceives.

The vine, absorbing by its leaves, a much greater portion of its nutritive principles than by its roots, these leaves and branches, if left, would absorb a much greater portion of sap than the heat would elaborate, and hence would result the immaturity of the grape. The same principles will not apply in a hotter climate, and a drier season and soil; and hence, in the most southern districts of France, and in Spain, Italy, and Sicily, these operations are not performed.

A third operation, the removal of the larger leaves, when the grape has attained almost its full size, has, besides the above, another object in view, which is, the exposure of the bunches to the ripening influence of the sun's rays. This is only necessary, or advantageous, in colder climates, it being seen above, that it is in some cases advantageous to ripen the grapes in the shade.

Where these operations are advantageous, much care and judgment is necessary to direct them. The branches should never be shortened before the vine has flowered, nor indeed before the grapes are formed.

The neglect of this precaution, by causing the reflux of the sap, and carrying a superabundance of it to the flower, at a delicate crisis, is one of the most frequent causes of its sterility. If too great a number of the leaves be removed, the grapes dry and rot, without reaching maturity; and this is not all, for the shoots which are still green, cease to ripen; and the buds, not having received, on the part of the leaves, their complement of vegetation, are either entirely barren the year; or, if they open into flowers, are unproductive of fruit.

CHAPTER FIFTH.

Of Labouring and Manuring the Soil for Vines.

THE advantage of labouring the soil, where vines are planted, has been recognised in every wine district, and its value appreciated, not only as disposing the soil for the more free circulation of air and moisture, and making it more penetrable for the numerous fibres of the roots, but also, as destroying that numerous tribe of parasitical plants, which spring up in all places where the greatest care is not taken to eradicate them.

These weeds, besides depriving the plant of a part of those juices which it ought to appropriate, and often keeping around it a degree of humidity, which exposes it to danger from the frosts of autumn, frequently send forth emanations, with which the fruit is imbued so strongly, as not to be freed from it by fermentation, the wine retaining a disagreeable, and often repugnant taste, which is generally imputed to other causes.

Though very frequent labours are considered dangerous, three diggings or hoeings, are conceived to be absolutely necessary; and, in particular cases, a fourth is advantageous.

Where the climate will admit of autumn pruning, it is recommended to give the first turning over immediately after it and thus carry to the roots, that refreshment which is necessary after the heats of the summer.

When the pruning is delayed till spring, the first labour should be delayed till it is finished, but should follow t immediately; that, before the opening of the buds, that freshness which exists in soil newly turned over, and which might induce frosts and endanger them, may be dissipated. The second labour should take place when the fruit is formed; and the third, which is generally a mere scraping of the surface, to destroy weeds, when it begins to ripen.

The depth to which the ground is turned over, is different, according to the differences of soil. At the base of hills, and on strong soils, it may be dug to the depth of six or seven inches, while, on very light soils, and on the summits of hills, the half of that depth will suffice. The practice of laying bare the roots of the plants, by forming a ridge between the rows, which prevails in some places before the winter, is severely reprobated, especially in colder climates, where, to expose the roots to the action of the frost, must be injurious.

Far from disturbing the roots in the tillage of the soil, the instrument should rather scrape the surface close to the stock, than penetrate near them. The roots from the inferior part of the plant, penetrate beyond the reach of the instrument; but those slender filaments, which come almost to the surface, are the most precious to the plant; and the destruction of these, by frequent and careless labouring, often causes a young and vigorous vine, to pass to a languishing and decaying state. The ground should be turned up in a direction transverse to the rows, and each operation should be in a manner opposite to the preceding; of course, this is understood only where the plough is not used; but this, though attended with more danger, and executing the work more imperfectly, and though, besides, proscribed by writers on the subject, is, consistently with my own knowledge, much used in many very excellent wine districts. The plough is worked by a pair of oxen, yoked by the horns, and muzzled, to prevent them from eating the foliage and fruit, of which they are remarkably fond. Several kinds of instruments of labour are described, as the spade, several sorts of hoes, and forks, &c. but those most in use are, an instrument, which I might describe, by comparing it to a small light spade, bent at one-third of its length from the top, to an angle of about 65°, with the handle; and an instrument of the same form, but having three prongs instead of being solid. This latter is more useful when, as frequently happens in vineyards, the soil is stoney.

The effects of manure, have been generally stated in a former chapter. It is, however, necessary, that soils, long under the same cultivation, should have their exhausted principles in some degree renewed; besides, the too luxuriant vegetation, which results from the employment of fresh and undecomposed manures, they frequently impart to the fruit, and still more to the wine, a disagreeable taste. By repeated and careful analyses of wines, produced by vineyards which were manured with sea-weed, pure muriate of soda was detected in them.

The principles of substances, employed as manure, being thus imbibed by the fruit, and developed in the wine, it is necessary that none containing injurious principles should be employed. In the best vineyards, when an amendment is given, it consists only of vegetable earth; and this, if it can be procured, should always be mixed with any dung that may be employed. Vegetable substances, such as mosses, leaves, &c. when decomposed, form an excellent amendment; as also, alluvial matter, deposited by rivers, lakes, &c. and when these milder applications cannot be procured, the stronger manures should be allowed to ferment, and to lose, as much as possible, of their carbonic acid. It is better to manure, in one year, only one part of the vineyard, and its injurious effects on the quality of the wine, are thus less observable. Different sorts of manure are also applied to different soils: and thus, when they tend to stiffness, an amendment frequently consists of sand, especially when mixed with shells, and other calcareous matter. Besides, the emanations from plants growing in the vineyards, and the principles imbibed from substances employed as manure, the neighbourhood of a lime kiln, of a charcoal furnace, or of any establishment where sea coal is consumed, is sufficient to give the wine a disagreeable taste, although it is not observable in the fruit before fermentation.

The capillary tubes of some kinds of the vine, frequently take up, also, very minutely divided parts of the predominant earth, and give to the wine a taste, flavour, or perfume, characteristic of it. Thus, the taste of the soil, "*goût de terroir*," is frequently a virtue, as in that called *gun flint*, "*pierre de fusil*," and sometimes disagreeable, as when aluminous. These latter, and many other tastes in the wine, are inherent in the nature of the soil; and it is to this that many delicious wines owe their peculiarities. When it is of an agreeable nature, it is more frequently called "*bouquet.*" Such are independent of the will and labour of man; but it is in his power to remove many of those which are owing to offensive effluvia in the air, whether arising from growing plants, or rank manures, or the impregnations of the atmosphere with sooty exhalations.

CHAPTER SIXTH.

Of the Diseases and Accidents incident to Vines, with the Means of Prevention, Remedy, and Renewal.

THE injuries to which the vine is liable, are not every where of the same nature, nor do they occur to the same extent, in all wine countries. In warmer climates, where frosts are rare, where the temperature of the atmosphere permits a wider plantation, and where vegetation is vigorous, without the abundance of the sap proving an obstacle to the maturity of the fruit, the vine is secure from those disasters to which a more severe climate subject it; at the same time, that it lessens its power of supporting them.

The principal injuries which it suffers, are occasioned by the intemperance of the seasons. These are, the destruction of the fruit buds, by the late frosts of spring, and the *running* of the flower*.

---

* The French call running, " *coulure ;*" the derangement of the parts of fructification, by whatever cause, which prevent the

As to lacerations of the roots, and bruises of the stock, they ought to be attributed to the carelessness, or unskilfulness of the workmen. The voracity of insects is the cause of others.

It would appear, that what are most to be dreaded of these evils, viz. the freezing of the buds, and the running of the flower, are beyond the effectual remedy of the cultivator, or that means of prevention have not yet been discovered, which are generally applicable, or which can be applied without swallowing up profit in expense. Such, indeed, is the report which was uniformly made to me, at a period*, when I had an opportunity of witnessing the destructive effects of frost, to such a high degree, that a proprietor of vines, who ought to have made 200 tons of wine, assured me that the frosts had not left him ten.

Writers on the vine recommend, when frost is dreaded, that heaps of straw, bad hay, and dried weeds, should be placed at intervals on that side of the vineyard which faces the rising sun; and that these, at his rising, should be lighted in such a way, that the smoke should intercept his rays. This is said to have been practised by M. Jurnilhac,

---

stamina and pistils from performing their functions, and consequently makes the flowers abortive.

* April, 1822.

and that part of the vineyard with which the means had been used was saved, while not a bud was left unfrosted in the unprotected part. If the dew has not made its appearance towards the middle of the night, it is considered a certain prognostic of frost. However, in the instance recorded, after the vineyard had several nights escaped the frost, the person left to watch, supposed he saw the dew an hour before sunrise, and, satisfied with this appearance, neglected to fire the heaps; the consequence was, that the whole was frozen.

It may well be supposed, that so clumsy, and, as it would be in many cases, so expensive a process, even had it succeeded in the experiment by which it is recommended, would not be generally adopted; and, accordingly, I have always found, that the prevention of injury by frost, was considered beyond the power of man.

The same may be said as to the *running*, so far as the seasons are the cause. The tenuity of the parts of fructification, require the finest weather for their favourable operation. A continuance of wet or cold weather, which prevents their developement; dry and hot weather, by which they are parched and withered; or severe gales, which separate them violently, and carry them to a distance; all act unfavourably, in preventing the sexual intercourse, and consequently rendering the flower abortive. But it often happens, that after the impregnation has taken place, and the fruit is formed, it detaches itself from the little footstalks which attach it to the bunch, and disappears. This is the effect of a vegetation too active, or sap too abundant. The sap, carried with violence and rapidity to the very delicate parts of the bunch, does not give time to the embryo fruit to appropriate it, but forces them off as it were by the effect of a spontaneous impulsion, and replaces them by changing and prolonging itself into wood. This theory is proved to be correct, by carefully making an outlet for the sap, on the wood bearing a new shoot, in such a way, that the wood may not be injured, and that the sap may not flow too quickly, which is done by carefully cutting off a small piece of bark, and replacing it with a piece of thread; the shoot close to it, will bring its grapes to perfection, although all the others on the same plant should prove abortive, and this, because the force of the sap was diminished by the operation. Unhappily, this requires a degree of minuteness, which makes it inapplicable on a large scale, but it points out the caution which ought to be exercised, in stopping the shoots, at the critical season of the vines flowering.

The vine, though uninjured by the frost or

running, frequently indicates, by the aspect of its leaves and fruit, that it suffers in some of its parts. This unhealthiness may arise from a variety of circumstances; as, the having been pruned at an improper time, or unskilfully, the shoot not having been taken off close to the old wood. It may, though in general vigorous, be unhealthy in some part, which may have been injured by the hail, (and this ought to be removed above the injury,) or by the tie which bound it to the pole not having been removed before the winter, and thus allowing the snow to lodge, and cause clefts and ulcers, which ought to have been removed at the time of pruning.

An excess of nourishment is frequently the cause of unhealthiness in the vine. When fresh dung, containing an abundance of viscous matter is spread on the soil, it is taken up by the capillary tubes, in such abundance, as to obstruct the canals of the sap, and the vine languishes by a sort of indigestion. The remedy in this case is, to spread a quantity of rubbish or sand on the soil, to correct its over richness.

When a vine has been propagated by a layer, it also frequently happens, that the decaying parts of the old wood still connected with it, furnish a sort of morbid sap which is most injurious to it. In this case, it is necessary to dig to the roots and remove the cause of the evil, as well as any of the roots which may seem to have suffered from it.

Notwithstanding the care of the workman, it often happens, that the stock is wounded by his instrument, and the sap, bleeding from the wound, is the cause of the languishing state of the plant. This is remedied by a plaster of clay, or soot, mixed with soft soap; if this is not sufficient, a cautery of hot iron is sometimes applied; and, if all other means should fail, in stopping the course of the sap, the wound should be cleaned, and the moisture removed by a sponge, after which, a plaster of pitch, spread on a piece of bladder, is tied firmly upon it.

Having escaped the intemperance of the seasons, and the unskilfulness, or carelessness of the cultivator, the vine has yet to fear the effects of insects gnawing its roots, or preying on its fruits or foliage. The principal of these are, a sort of caterpillar, called, from its preference to the vine, vine-worm, and several sorts of insects which, in the state of larvæ, subsist at the expense of the roots; or, in their perfect state, cut the tender shoot half through, that the leaves, in which they deposit their eggs, may be more pliable; or pierce the leaves with holes as numerous as those of a riddle: and the common garden snail, whose mischief is not confined to the leaves and buds it destroys, for wherever it has left its slime, the transpiration of the leaf is stopt.

The egg of the *vine-worm* is supposed to be deposited by the butterfly, in the berry, at a very early stage of its existence. The puncture made by it is extremely minute, and sometimes pierces the stone to a considerable depth. The environs of the puncture, are of a bluish colour, the skin smooth, and beneath this skin the pulp is changed to a hard substance. The insect is developed in, and at first nourished at, the expense of the berry, where the egg is deposited, but by and by, it visits the neighbouring berries of the bunch, and establishes a communication between them, by a sort of thread which it spins. This, next to wet weather, is one of the principal causes of the rotting of the fruit; and if the bunch has only in part rotted, the silky web of the worm may generally be traced about the decayed grapes. The extreme minuteness of this insect, and the agility of its motions, make its destruction a very difficult matter. When the insects, which are called *cut buds*, from their cutting the shoot half through, have deposited their eggs in the leaves, which may be distinguished by being curled or rolled up, it is generally well worth the trouble, to cut the leaves off and have them burned.

Different means, in different parts of the world, are employed, to prevent the attacks of various sorts of insects The method recommended by Cato, *(de re rustica)* is still practised throughout Greece. In consists in surrounding the stock with a mixture of pitch, sulphur, and oil*. The proprietors of the vineyards of Constantia, employ a means which serves to shew the minute care which their valuable produce will allow to be lavished upon them. This is, to suspend a bunch of vine leaves, dipt in brandy, below each bunch of grapes

Those injuries which the roots may sustain from grubs, admit of several means of prevention. The grubs are always to be found at a certain depth in the soil, where they bury themselves, to escape equally from the heat and the cold. If, during the winter, the ground is dug up, many of them are sure to perish. Their preference for leguminous plants, is also taken advantage of for their destruction. A row of these is sown between the rows of vines, and when their sickly state shew that the grubs have assembled at their roots, they are dug up, and thus destroyed. During the winter too, they are collected by the heat

---

* *Topography de Vignobles.*

arising from small heaps of dung. In some wine countries, the snail is accounted such a delicacy, that its collection is rather a matter of profit than than expense.

The most careful cultivator frequently finds himself under the necessity of replacing plants which may have perished by divers accidents, or by old age, and it is frequently his interest to substitute a variety which may be more fitted to the climate or soil.

The method of propagating by layers, is resorted to in the first case, and recourse may be had to grafting in the second. In grafting vines, it is recommended, that the stock should be cut two inches below the surface of the soil, and it is generally done, by what English gardeners call cleft grafting. The scions are cut at the end of autumn, and preserved carefully through the winter, in the way prescribed for cuttings. When the sap begins to circulate, the stock, which should be sound, is cut clean, in a horizontal direction, and cleft in the middle, in a space without a knot. Some recommend, that the scions, previous to insertion, should be immersed a few hours in water. The scion should be the lowest part of a shoot, and should be cut down to three eyes or knots. It is usual to put two scions in one stock; they are carefully cut in the form of a wedge, having an acuter angle on the internal edge, and the outer edge touching the bark of the stock over as large a surface as possible. The first, or lowest eye, should coincide with the stock; the second, be at the surface of the soil; and the uppermost, altogether out of the soil. It should then be carefully bound, and covered with soil, to protect it from the sun's rays. Cloudy and moist weather is most favourable for the operation. Scorching suns, parching winds, and heavy rains, are equally unfavourable. Grafting succeeds well on all soils, excepting in such as are very stoney and acid, or in such as have very little depth; in these, the sun generally scorches and withers the scion before it has taken.

The sap circulates so freely in the whole wood of the vine, that, if the operation be performed with only ordinary care, it is sure to succeed, and, if it succeeds well, it will give strong shoots, and may be pruned to a considerable length the second year.

The common method of filling an empty space by a layer, is to choose, from the best of the neighbouring vines, a long shoot, and sink it to a sufficient depth, in a trench between its stock and where it is to grow. It is there fixed to a support, and pruned to two or three eyes. The depth to which it should be sunk, will vary according to the nature of the soil; but in all cases, it should be so far below the surface, as that its roots may escape the instrument of the workman. If it has succeeded well, its connection with the parent stock may be dissolved towards the end of summer. Its remaining too long connected with the parent stock proves injurious to it, as may be seen by its casting its leaves earlier in the ensuing season, than the neighbouring plants. Indeed, this practice is much condemned, and it is recommended, that instead of one shoot being laid, the whole stock should be converted into a layer to furnish young plants. A trench, from sixteen to twenty inches in depth, is made close up to the foot of the stock, and the intervening roots being detached, it is laid horizontally into it, the shoots or branches being dressed against the sides of it, and covered with soil, some fresh mould being generally added. A great number of young plants is thus procured, which may be planted in vacant spaces, without danger of being choked by the roots and branches of the surrounding plants, as would be too generally the case, were cutting employed. It is recommended, that the support given to the young plant should be of old wood, from which the bark is detached; poles of osier, or other young wood, nourish within their bark swarms of insects, and sometimes take root, and are injurous to the roots of the plant when pulled up. The juices of the decaying bark, too, carried down by the rain, are also injurious, and sometimes destructive to the vine; and this observation is applicable in all cases, as well as in that of the young plant. The season for laying, is the same as that for planting.

The old age of a vineyard—the approaching epoch of its destruction, is announced by the feebleness of its shoots, by the smallness of its leaves, and by the scarcity and diminutive size of its fruits. When a vineyard has, for two or three successive years, ceased to indemnify the proprietor, and its sterility cannot be imputed to the inclemency of the weather, nor to the ravages of insects, nor to the defects of culture, it must be attributed to old age. But, before its extirpation, a plan has frequently been adopted, and always with success, in those countries where the climate will not allow a large and wide growth; this is, to take out each alternate plant. The roots of those which are left, take insensibly the place of those which have been removed, and a more abundant sap is supplied, without danger of its being less matured, as the canals of the sap are, from age, no longer capable of being injuriously dilated. A vineyard has thus gradually recovered its vigour, and the produce of one-half the number of plants exceeded that of the whole, without a deterioration of the quality.

From the superior excellence of the wine of old stocks, it is always with regret that they are removed. Vineyards of the greatest celebrity, have lost much of their reputaion, by being replanted; and hence, in some districts, when vines tend to old age, a certain proportion of young plants is annually introduced, and the change of the produce thus rendered less observable.

The treatment of the vine, for the production of grapes for the table, is described in every book of English gardening. I shall, therefore, refrain from going into particulars relative to it. The object in this case is, to obtain as large a produce as is possible, without being injurious to the tree. That sort of maturity, which is necessary for the production of saccharine matter, is also of no importance, as it is not requisite in any great degree, to give a very sweet or agreeable taste to the grape; and a well manured border, and a length of pruning, proportioned to the nourishment afforded, may be taken advantage of, without much danger of the quantity of produce being injurious to its quality.

I shall, therefore, close this part of the work, with some very brief notices, of the best methods of preserving grapes fresh, and of making what we call raisins.

The perfect maturity of the grape is known by the hardening of the stalk, and the brown colour it assumes, indicating that the sap has ceased to flow to it.

A dry day, when there is much sunshine, is chosen, in which to cut the grapes, when each bunch is carefully examined, and any berries that are in a decayed state, or over ripe, removed. A quantity of dry moss is then spread over a hurdle, and the bunches laid on it, in such a way, that they may not touch. The hurdles are carefully removed under cover, in the evening. If, on the following day, the weather is fine, and the sun's rays not intercepted by clouds, the hurdles should be carried out, and the grapes exposed to the sun's rays. After two or three hours, the bunches are carefully turned, and when they are thus freed from all external moisture, they are restored to the fruit-house. The common method is then to attach them to strings, and hang them up in a dry place, where there is little circulation of air. Some fix them by the higher part of the stalk, and each individual grape is thus isolated, and prevented from pressing and injuring its neighbour. It is not uncommon to have good grapes by this method, when it is carefully conducted, seven or eight months after the vintage.

Other methods are, by removing the fruit from the contact of the air. Take a box, of any convenient size, and suspend in it, by pins and cards, as many bunches as it will hold without pressing. Close it hermetically, by plastering the junctures with lime, place it in a dry place, and cover it with a few inches of fine sand. Grapes are kept in this way in perfect preservation, but it is necessary to use them very soon after the box is opened.

Others are dipped repeatedly in a lie made of the finely sifted ashes of burnt shoots, and then packed in boxes with the dry ashes. When they are to be used, they are plunged in water, and the adhering matter easily parts from them; others are packed in clean chaff, and this also seems to answer the purpose.

Raisins are prepared in two ways. Those called sun raisins are allowed to adhere to the vine, after the stalk is cut half through, to stop the circulation of the sap; and, after the sun has candied them, they are packed in boxes. Those called Lexia raisins, are cut off from the vine, and after being dipped in a lie (Lexia) of the ashes of vine shoots, are carefully dried in the sun.

PART SECOND.

CHAPTER FIRST.

Of the most favourable period for the Vintage, and the Method of Procedure.

IT has been established as a principle, that the time of the vintage is that of the maturity of the grape, since in this state it yields, by fermentation, the greatest possible quantity of alcohol. But this general principle is subject to several exceptions; for, in the colder climates, the grape seldom attains its perfect maturity, and it is necessary that it should be gathered in a comparatively green state, to save it from the putrefaction to which it would be exposed by the prevalence of cold moist weather, towards the end of autumn. The object, in such climates, is then to seize the moment when it ceases to gain more ripeness on the stock.

There are, besides, countries where the wine is esteemed for qualities with which the perfect maturity of the grape is incompatible It is often an object to obtain wine rather endowed with an agreeable flavour, than rich in alcohol; but this flavour is dissipated when the grape is perfectly ripe. It frequently happens, also, that it is an object to obtain brisk wines, and this quality is only developed, when grapes not absolutely ripe are employed.

It appears, then, impossible to lay down a general rule, by which to determine, constantly and invariably, the time of the vintage; it depends upon the end proposed, and on the climate in which the vine is situated; and it is from experience alone, that in each district, the fittest time in each year can be determined.

Even the perfect maturity of the grapes does not afford an invariable rule, as in many places they are allowed to dry upon the stock, for the purpose of concentrating the saccharine principle, and producing a sweet wine.

It has been observed, with truth, that if all the cultivator's intelligence and care have been necessary, in bringing his grapes thus far, this is no time to relax his industry, the management of the vintage being his most difficult task. It is to the well perceived necessity of directing and watching over all its operations, that is to be referred the custom, so general, of abandoning the cities at its approach.

The time is not far removed, when, in the most

celebrated wine districts of France, the epoch of the vintage was announced with solemnity, and celebrated by public rejoicings. The magistrates, accompanied by the most intelligent and experienced agriculturists of the neighbourhood, visited the vineyards of the different cantons, to judge of the maturity of the grape, and no proprietor was allowed to proceed with his vintage, till permission was solemnly proclaimed. The reputation which the wines of the district enjoyed, was considered public property; and these precautions were taken, that no unskilful or careless proprietor might injure this reputation, by the mismanagement of his own wines.

This system of forcing a man to do well, in spite of himself, has passed away; and, whatever opinion may be formed, of the soundness of the principles on which such regulations were formed, their having existed, proves, at least, how much it has always been accounted a matter of importance and difficulty, to determine aright the period of the vintage.

In a great majority of cases, this period is that at which the grape has attained its maturity, and this maturity may be ascertained by the reunion of the following signs:—

1st, The stalk of the bunch changes its colour from green to brown.

2d, The bunch becomes pendant.

3d, The berry has lost its hardness, and the skin has become thin and translucent.

4th, The berries are easily, and without effort, detached from the bunch.

5th, The juice of the grape has become savoury, sweet, thick, and viscid.

6th, The stones or seeds of the berry, are free from any glutinous substance.

The falling of the leaves, announces rather the return of the winter, than the maturity of the fruit; it is, therefore, considered rather equivocal, as well as the rotting of the grapes, which a thousand causes may decide, without allowing any proof of maturity to be drawn from them. Nevertheless, when frost has caused the falling of the leaf, it is no longer safe to delay the vintage. The grapes, especially the black varieties, are not capable of receiving further maturation; a longer stay on the stock would only decide their putrefaction. In very hot climates, however, where the atmosphere preserves a great degree of dryness, and where, consequently, the grape, arrived at perfect maturity, dries upon the stock, and acquires the property of giving a more spirituous and sweeter wine, the vintage may be without danger delayed.

There are qualities in wine, which can only be obtained, by allowing the grapes which are to furnish it, to dry upon the stock; thus, at Rivesaltes, where the best sweet wines of France are made, the grapes are dried before they are gathered. The same system is pursued with regard to those from which the sweet wines of Cyprus and Candia are made, as well as the celebrated Tokay, and many of the Italian sweet wines. The wines of Arbois and Chateau Chalons, are made from grapes, which are not gathered till December. In Touraine, and elsewhere, the *vin de paille* is made, by gathering the grapes in dry weather, and exposing them on hurdles to the sun's rays, after which, the decayed berries are carefully removed, and they are pressed and fermented.

When, from the state of the fruit, the commencement of the vintage is determined upon, it is still advisable to delay proceeding, till the settled state of the weather promises uninterrupted labours. It is recommended, also, that the soil should be dry, as well as the fruit, and that the dews of the morning should be dissipated, experience having proved, that, when the grapes are gathered during cold weather, the fermentation proceeds more slowly, and with more difficulty, than when gathered under contrary circumstances.

It is of importance, also, that all the grapes which are to compose a vat, should be gathered under the same temperature; and, where this is impossible, they should be kept in a warm place till an equal temperature is acquired. The advantage of having the mass uniformly in a state of fermentation throughout, is the reason for this, and the same principle points out the advantage of having such a number of vintagers as shall complete a vat in one day.

The method most generally practised, is to sever the bunch with the thumb nail; in some places a pruning knife is made use of for the purpose, but a pair of good scissors is recommended, in preference to either of these modes. The stalk should be cut as near the bunch as possible, and great care should be used in rejecting such as have decayed, and leaving such as are unripe.

In countries where they are jealous of the quality of their wines, the grapes are gathered at different times. The first vat resulting from the first gathering, is always the best. The grapes are better nourished, the berries of each bunch more equal, and the maturity more perfect through the mass. Besides, the first choice is always of grapes which have reached an earlier maturity, in consequence of having been better exposed to the sun; and for this reason, the wine resulting from their fermentation should be superior.

These precautions are only neglected, where

the wine, under the best management, is inferior in quality, or when it is intended for distillation.

When it is determined to make a choice of grapes, the following directions may guide in making it:—Not to cut any but those which have been well exposed to the sun's rays, and of which the berries are equally large, and equally coloured; to reject all which have been in the shade, and such as have been close to the ground; and to prefer the lowest bunches of a shoot.

In the vineyards which furnish the different descriptions of Bordeaux wine, much care is used in picking the grapes; and so minute is this operation in some cantons, that the vintage lasts for two months, and the grapes are picked at six different times. In some districts it is conceived, that the wine, made from grapes which are all ripe, is too sweet, and a portion of sourer grapes are intentionally mixed with them. Again, there are countries where the grape, never reaching a state of absolute maturity, and consequently not developing that portion of saccharine principle necessary to the formation of alcohol, is, nevertheless, gathered before the appearance of frost, because, at this time, it contains a sort of sharp acid principle, which gives a peculiar character to the wine. In such countries, it is observed, that this quality disappears when the grape reaches a higher degree of maturity.

As it is of great importance to the regularity of the fermentation, that the grapes should be kept entire till pressed, great care should be taken not to load the baskets too heavily. In some districts, where the grapes are gathered very ripe, each vintager carries a small basket, which is emptied into large casks or tubs, placed on a cart, to be transported to the wine cellar. In Burgundy, when the wine cellar is distant from the vineyard, the grapes are pressed into casks which are closed, and thus conveyed to it; but this would be dangerous, were not the vat filled in one day. By these means, the juice of any grapes which may be crushed, (and the finest are most liable to be so), is preserved. When the grapes are less ripe, large baskets are generally employed; these are placed on carts or horses, according to local circumstances. In Champagne, the baskets are carefully wrapt round with cloths, to keep out the heat of the sun, whose rays might cause a premature and unequal fermentation; they are then kept in the shade till the evening.

CHAPTER SECOND.

Of the means of disposing the Juice of the Grape to Fermentation.

To the liberality of nature we are indebted for the grape, but it is the art of man, in submitting its juices to fermentation, which gives us wine.

The method of submitting the grapes to fermentation, varies, according to their qualities, in different countries; or, the degree of maturity to which they arrive, in different seasons, in the same country; or, to the particular description of wine most in request.

Pliny *(de Bico vino apud Græcos clarissimo)* informs us, that for this wine, the grape was gathered a little before its maturity, and exposed to the rays of an ardent sun, during three days, being turned three times a day, and on the fourth day its juice was expressed.

The ancients were also acquainted with the method of digesting or concentrating the must, as appears by their having three kinds of concentrated wine. The first, called *passum*, was made from grapes dried in the sun; the second, *defrutum*, was obtained by reducing the must one-half, by means of fire; and the third, named *sapa*, from must, concentrated to such a degree, that only one-third of the original quantity remained.

Several methods of concentrating the juices of the white grape, by allowing it to wither on the stock, or, after being cut, to dry in the sun, have been mentioned in a former chapter, as being the practice in various countries at the present day; and in treating of fermentation, it shall be shewn, that it may be advantageously directed by thickening a part of the must to mix with the remainder; and that a degree of strength is thus given to wines, which they would never attain without it. What is chiefly to be treated of in this chapter, is the separation of the grapes from the stalks, and treading them.

The advantages and disadvantages of these processes, called in France, *egrappage* and *foulage*, have given rise to considerable discussion among those who have treated of the subject; but the question, on both sides, seems to have been, like many others, treated in too exclusive a manner, as will appear by placing it in its true point of view.

The stalks, being possessed of a bitter principle and austere taste, communicate to the wine, with which they have been allowed to ferment, these qualities, in a greater or less degree; but there are wines produced in cold and wet countries, so weak and insipid, that their flatness is rather agreeably relieved by the slight asperity derived from the stalk, and it has been found to give durability to wines which, without it, would speedily degenerate into ropiness. This was found to be the case in the Orleanois; when, in consequence of the published opinions of writers on this subject, they commenced the *egrappage*; but, in consequence of finding that the wine made without the stalk sooner altered, they returned to their old practice. It has also been ascertained by experience, that the fermentation proceeds with more force and regularity, when the stalks are left in the must; and, in this point of view, they may be considered as an advantageous ferment, in all cases where there is reason to fear a slow or incomplete fermentation.

In the neighbourhood of Bordeaux, all the red grapes, which produce the best wine, are deprived of a portion of their stalks, and this portion is determined by the degree of maturity they have reached. When the fruit is not perfectly ripe, or has been touched by the frost before the vintage, they deprive it of a greater proportion; while, when it is very ripe, they leave a greater quantity, to facilitate the fermentation, and prevent the too great sweetness of the wine. White grapes are not deprived of their stalks, when submitted to fermentation.

Thus, though the stalks can neither add to the spirituosity of the wine nor its perfume, because they are destitute of saccharine matter, and aroma, their slight asperity may advantageously correct the insipidity of some wines; and, by facilitating fermentation, they concur towards a more complete decomposition of the must, and to the production of a greater quantity of alcohol.

Before quitting this part of the subject, wines may be considered in two points of view, viz. whether intended for drinking, or for distillation; qualities are required in the former, which are superfluous in the latter. Thus, in making wines for distillation, the object is, to procure the greatest possible quantity of alcohol, without regard to other qualities; while, in the latter, the taste and flavour of the wine, are equally objects of request. In the former case, the must may be fermented with all the stalks; in the latter case, it is a consideration of the first importance, how far the quantity of stalks, fermented in the must, will affect the wine, with regard to its taste and perfume, as well as its spirituosity; and experience of the qualities of his grapes, and the taste of the consumers of his wine, can alone determine the cultivator what proportion of these properties his wine may most advantageously possess.

The effects of the stalk, then, being to facilitate the fermentation, and give durability to the wine, while it gives it a taste rather harsh and rough, it may be said to be generally advantageous, and sometimes necessary, to allow them to remain in the must of grapes, produced in a cold or moist climate; while in warmer latitudes, where the wine is naturally more generous, and not in need of the qualities imparted by them, their being allowed to ferment with, or being picked from, the fruit, should be determined by the intention, in making the wine for drinking or distillation. Their remaining in the former case, may deprive the wine of much of that flavour and perfume so highly valued, while their deprivation cannot much injure the wine, in regard to its strength and durability. But, in the latter case, the end in view is best attained by suffering them to remain.

The operation is generally performed with a branch, having three prongs, in the shape of a triangular fork:—one prong is thrust to the bottom of the tub, or bucket, containing the grapes, and the other two moved rapidly round, till all the berries are detached, when the stalks are taken off with the hand. A riddle made of osier twigs is also employed for this purpose.

But whether it is determined that the stalks shall ferment with the grapes, or be taken out, the advantage of treading them, in all cases, has never been called in question. This operation generally takes place as they arrive from the vineyard, though, for the reasons stated in a preceding chapter, it would be better to submit them all to it at the same time; and this remark is more particularly applicable, in situations where the grape, owing to climate, or other causes, is not rich in saccharine matter, and, consequently, not capable of undergoing a lengthened fermentation.

A sort of case, or cage, is provided, made of bars of wood: it is open above, and about two feet in height, and four in width; the intervals are sufficiently wide to allow the expressed juice to escape, but close enough to retain the entire fruit; this is placed above the vat, where it is supported by two beams resting against its sides. Into this the fruit is emptied, and a man, leaning upon the beams, continues to jump and dance upon it with large wooden shoes, till all the grapes are broken; after which, a sliding bar, in one of the sides, is drawn, and the skins and stones pushed into the vat or out of the vat, according to the intention of allowing them to ferment with the must or not.

No sooner is the cage cleared, than another supply of grapes is furnished, and the operation is continued, till the vat is full, or the vintage concluded.

In the central districts of France, and in all those where I have had an opportunity of personally examining the wine cellars, instead of the method above described, a stage is raised above the level of the vat, and inclining towards it; and the cellars, being frequently on the side of a hill, there is an entrance to this stage from the side opposite to the door, through which the grapes are carried, and the operation carried on as in the other case, the must running by a spout into the vat, or into a reservoir, from which it is conveyed to it. A different method is practised in some places, the grapes being put into the vat as soon as they arrive, are then slightly trod, and, when fermentation has commenced, the upper part of the liquor is carefully drained off, and allowed to finish its fermentation in casks; what remains, is submitted to the press, and yields a wine with more colour, and less perfume than the first.

In whatever way this operation is performed, Chaptal considers it of the greatest importance, that each berry should be broken, as the march of fermentation will only be uniform, in proportion as the operation is perfectly performed. The expressed juice shall have terminated the period of its decomposition, before the grapes, which have escaped the treading, shall have commenced theirs; and thus a mass be presented for fermentation, whose elements are not in affinity; but, when the grapes are uniformly pressed, the fermentation is spontaneous, and no partial movements obscure the signs by which it is announced, accompanied, or succeeded.

On the other hand, Labergerie* affirms, that these unbroken berries undergo a decomposition, in common with the rest of the mass, notwithstanding their spherical form; and that it would rather be disadvantageous, than otherwise, to crush every individual grape; as, when the must is in sufficient quantity, they operate most actively to the general shock of fermentation. "The manner of treading, in all districts," says he, "proves that they are useful, a few being always suffered to escape." In Burgundy, he has left a quantity of these entire grapes, which are there called *grumes*, (clods) in the proportion of one-fifth of the whole; when examined, after the vats were emptied, they were found entire, but destitute of vinous substance, deprived of their saccharine matter, and their colour quite gone; when broken by the tooth, they were harsh and ill tasted; when

---

* Cours de Agriculture, Paris, 1822.

pressed by the finger, they offered only their seeds, and fibrous filament.

After what has been already said, on the advantage of a uniform fermentation, it is unnecessary to urge the necessity of providing a sufficient number of vintagers, to fill a vat within 24 hours. It is, in fact, by an attention to these little circumstances, that the wines of one district, or country, excel those of another. In Italy, where the climate and soil are so favourable for the vine, that they could scarcely avoid making excellent wine, if the process were conducted with any regard to principles, the generality of the wines are of a very inferior description; and the method of conducting the vintage, is sufficient to account for it. The same vat is destined to receive the vintage of many days, each added to the mass collected before, till it is full. This is not unfrequently till fifteen days have elapsed. The produce of such a vat is, in fact, a medley of different wines, more or less fermented.

Although the vintage is usually conducted in the manner above described; the process of treading the grapes, and causing them to ferment in the vat, is by no means universal. The management of the brisk wines of Champagne, for example, is very different, and with a description of it, this chapter will be terminated.

In gathering the grapes, they carefully select the ripest and most sound, rejecting those which are decayed, dry, or broken. They are carried in large panniers on horseback to the cellar, the precaution being used, of wrapping a cloth round the basket, to guard against any fermentation which the sun's rays might excite. The baskets filled during the day, are placed in the evening under the press, which is charged according to its power, with from twenty to forty large baskets.*

---

* The screw press is generally employed, though in some cases the principle of the common lever is applied.

Much care is necessary in conducting the operation, as the application of too violent a pressure endangers the machinery. The wheel of the screw is worked by a vertical, or horizontal wheel, of larger or smaller dimensions, which is quite detached from it. The force should be applied gradually, and sufficient time allowed for the wine to run out.

When nothing more can be gained, the press is raised, and the edges of the marc, or husks, cut again into a square form, and what is cut off regularly built up above, when it is again pressed; and so on, as often as it shall be judged necessary. In small presses, it is sometimes repeated for the fifth time. Much of the success of the operation, depends upon the regularity with which the marc is built up in the press; it should never cover more than two-thirds of the surface, as it enlarges when pressed, and much of the wine might thus run over the edge and be lost. When the grapes have been freed from the stalks, it is necessary to use straw to raise them sufficiently; a layer of straw is placed round the edges on the bottom, and after the marc is a certain height, this is folded

The wine press having been previously well washed and wiped, and the screw, &c. greased, the grapes are subjected to three successive and rapid pressings. This operation of three pressings ought to be completed in an hour, when the workmen are habituated to the employment. The expressed juice is received in a smaller vat, whence it is carried to the vat in which it remains all night to subside. The wine produced from these three pressings, is called *vin d'élite*, wine of choice. Next morning, it is deposited in casks prepared for its reception, by being well vapoured with sulphur, and well rinced.

As there still remains must in the marc, it is subjected to another pressing, which is called the first cut, because the edges of the marc are cut off, and again placed immediately under the press.

The wine arising from this, is frequently mixed

---

over, and a new layer placed for the reception of more husks, and so on, to the height of the press.

The greatest possible cleanliness should be preserved throughout the place where the press and vats are situated, which is generally distinct from the cellar where the wines are kept; not only because a free circulation of air is necessary for the safety of the workmen, on account of the carbonic acid, but because the admission of heat is highly advantageous for the fermentation, both of which circumstances are unfavourable for a cellar where wines are kept.

with the wine of choice, a second, a third, and sometimes a fourth cut is given, but the wine from the latter is always stained and harsh.

When it is proposed to make pink wine, or rosé, a few of the stalks are taken from the grapes, and they are trod lightly, and allowed to enter into fermentation; they are then carried to the press, and subjected to the same pressings as for the white, but the wine resulting from them all, is mixed.

The white wine is no sooner deposited in the casks, than it forthwith enters into a tumultuous fermentation, which, however, soon degenerates into an insensible fermentation.

Towards the end of December, it ceases to ferment, and becomes clear. It is then decanted, and clarified with isinglass, in the proportion of half an ounce to fifty gallons. A month or six weeks afterwards, there is another movement of fermentation, when it is again decanted, and clarified with half the quantity. It remains in this state till March, at which time it is bottled. All these manipulations should take place in clear and frosty weather.

The fermentation not having entirely ceased when the wine is bottled, it frequently happens, during the autumn, that it bursts the bottles.

It is not till eighteen months after bottling, that the fermentation has entirely ceased, at which time it is taken from the bottles, to be relieved from the sediment it has deposited.

When all these operations have been carefully conducted, the white wine of Champagne is in no danger of altering for fifteen or twenty years.

CHAPTER THIRD.

Of the Phenomena of Fermentation, and the means of managing it.

SCARCELY is the must deposited in the vat, when fermentation commences. The juice which runs from the grape, in consequence of the pressure or jolting it receives in the carriage from the vineyard, may even be seen fermenting before it reaches the wine cellar. It was the practice of the ancients, to separate, with care, the first running, which only came from the ripest grapes, and cause it to ferment separately; and this is still occasionally practised, when a very delicate and slightly coloured wine is desired. But this forms only a small share of what the grapes yield, and is generally mixed with the produce of the treading, and allowed to ferment with it.

The vats in which the fermentation takes place, are constructed sometimes of wood and sometimes of stone, and are of a capacity proportioned to the produce of the vineyard. Those constructed of masonry, are usually of dressed stone, and are sometimes lined with brick and cement. Each kind has its partizans. If the vats of wood are more frequently in need of repair, and more liable to be affected by changes of atmosphere, their deficiency is more easily observed and remedied, and they are free from that constant chillness incident to those of stone.

In a very warm climate, the question may be determined by the cheapness of materials; but in colder climates, where artificial heat is sometimes necessary to aid the fermentation, wood alone should be employed.

Before the must is deposited in the vat, it should be cleansed with the greatest care, and well rubbed with warm water; and when it is of stone, it is usual to inclose it with two or three coats of lime. In Burgundy, where the vats are all of wood, it is customary, after washing with hot water, to pass a small quantity of brandy over the interior.

The ancients considered the preparation of the vat of the greatest importance; not only was it rubbed with different liquids, such as decoctions of aromatic plants, salt water, boiling must, &c. but smoked, by burning in it different perfumes.

As the whole process of vinification consists in the changes operated on the must, by the agency of fermentation, it is important to consider this subject under every point of view. We shall first, then, consider the causes which contribute to the vinous fermentation; then, after which, we shall examine its effects, or product; and conclude, by deducing, from actual experience, some general principles, to direct the cultivator in conducting it.

SECTION I.

Of the Causes which influence Fermentation.

OBSERVATION has taught us, that certain conditions are requisite in the must, in order to fermentation establishing itself, and following out its periods in a regular manner. A certain degree of heat, the contact of the air, the existence of a vegeto-animal, and of a saccharine principle in the must, are about the conditions considered requisite. We shall endeavour to explain what is due to each.

Temperature.

The temperature indicated by the 66th degree of Fahrenheit's thermometer, is generally considered the most favourable for the vinous fermentation. It languishes below this degree, and becomes too tumultuous above it.

It follows, from this, that, when the temperature of the place where the vat stands is below the 59th degree of Fahrenheit, it is necessary to raise it by artificial means; boiling must, may be mixed with the mass, to carry it to the proper temperature, and the cellar warmed with stoves to maintain it. In Burgundy, a cylinder such as is used for heating baths, is introduced into the vat. A phenomenon sufficiently extraordinary, but whose truth seems too well established by numerous observations to admit of doubt, is, that the fermentation is slow, in proportion as the atmosphere has been cold, at the moment of gathering the vintage. Rozier observed, in 1769, that grapes gathered on the 7th, 8th, and 9th October, remained in the vat till the 19th, without showing any disposition to ferment. The thermometer was two degrees below the freezing point in the mornings, and only rose three degrees above it during the days on which they were gathered. The fermentation was not completed till the 25th, while a vat full of must, from grapes of the same kind, gathered on the 16th, at a much higher temperature, had completed theirs on the 21st or 22d.

This fact merits much attention. It proves, that when must, in a very cold state, is deposited in a vat, it retains its temperature for a long time, and in a greater degree, if the temperature of the cellar where it is placed is cold. In such a case, the fermentation cannot but be slow and imperfect, but it may be assisted, by warming a part of the must, and pouring it into the vat, till the whole mass acquires a suitable temperature. It should be introduced by the bottom of the vat, and this is effected by a tunnel, having its inferior end closed with a bung, which can be drawn out when it has reached the bottom. The temperature of the cellar should, at the same time, be raised to the 59th degree of Fahrenheit.

It has been observed in Champagne, that grapes gathered in the morning, are longer of commencing to ferment, than those gathered after mid-day, and during sunshine and fogs; moist weather, and slight frosts, are so many causes which contribute to retard fermentation.

The result of some experiments made by Chaptal, are in accord with these observations, and even go to prove, that, when the low temperature of the fluid does not allow of its generating, in regular succession, all the phenomena of fermentation, it is very difficult completely to re-establish them by heat. He diluted a quantity of the *extract*, or essence of grapes, in water at a temperature seven degrees above the freezing point, and added a quantity of yeast, to assist the fermentation, which commenced quickly enough, when the temperature of the liquid was raised to the 64th degree of Fahrenheit, but very soon ceased.

An equal quantity of extract diluted, and kept at the temperature of 64°, during two days previous to the leaven being added, underwent a more regular and complete fermentation.

From what has been said, the following conclusions may be drawn:—

1st, That the grapes should be gathered in the heat, and the vintage not commenced till the rays of the sun have dissipated the dews of the night, and warmed the vine.

2d, That the quantity necessary to charge a vat, should be gathered in the shortest possible time.

3d, That, if the grapes are gathered in different states of the atmosphere, it is advantageous to put them in a warm place, or expose them to the sun's rays, till the whole mass takes an uniform temperature.

4th, That the temperature of the must ought, at least, to be 59° of Fahrenheit, and, when below that rate of temperature, should be brought to it by artificial heat.

5th, That the temperature of the cellar, should be at least 59 degrees, and uniform.

6th, That it is advantageous to place planks over the vats, on which cloths may be spread to preserve a uniform heat in the fermenting mass.

Atmospheric Air.

It had often been observed, that the process of fermentation might be moderated or retarded, by withdrawing the must from the direct action of the air, and keeping it under a cold temperature. And hence, some chemists have considered the air of the atmosphere as indispensable to fermentation. A more attentive examination of all the phenomena which the march of fermentation presents, will assist in giving due weight to all the opinions which have been advanced on this subject.

That the air is favourable to fermentation, there can be no doubt. This is a point established by the accordance of all the known facts connected with the subject, and without its contact, the must continues long without undergoing any change. But, it is equally certain, that though the must, deposited in close vessels, undergoes, very slowly, the process of fermentation, it terminates at length, and the wine resulting from it is even more generous than when fermented in contact with the air.

If a little of the yeast of beer and molasses, is diluted in water, and introduced into a flask with a bent neck, which is made to open under a bell full of water, inverted on the shelf of the pneumatic trough, at the temperature of 54° to 59°, the first phenomena of fermentation in a few minutes appear. The empty part of the flask is soon filled with bubbles and scum, and much carbonic acid passes into the bell; and these movements do not cease till the liquor has become vinous. In no case has it been observed, that there was an absorption of atmospheric air.

If, instead of allowing a free issue to the garous matters which escape during fermentation, their disengagement is opposed by conducting it in close vessels, then the fermentation slackens, and with difficulty, and, after a long time, it terminates its periods.

It appeared, from these facts, that the atmospheric air is not necessary to fermentation, since it took place in close vessels; but it was important to ascertain, whether the air bubbles dispersed through the fermentable fluid, or the couch of air above it might not contribute to this operation.

To ascertain this, M. Gay Lussac instituted an experiment, which has thrown the greatest light on the question. He introduced some very ripe grapes under an *eprouvette* of quicksilver; and, to drive away the small air bubbles adhering to the walls, he filled it successively, and at many relays, with carbonic acid and mercury. He then crushed the grapes with a tube, the surface of which he had freed from all globules of air, by agitation in the mercurial bath. To whatever degree the heat was raised, the must underwent no fermentation; but, while the heat was between 70° and 75°, he introduced some bubbles of oxygen gas, and in a few minutes, the fermentation was established to such a degree, that the bell was filled with carbonic acid.

It follows, from this fine experiment, that the first movement of fermentation is determined by the air, and that afterwards it continues without the aid of this external agent. The contact of some bubbles of air, determines a first combination of its oxygen with carbon; from that moment, the equilibrium among the constituent principles of the must is destroyed; their combination is imperfect, and nature is employed in forming new ones from them.

The air is, then, the first ferment which commences the decomposition of the must; the reaction of its constituent principles gives birth to new compounds, which change its primitive nature.

The air of the atmosphere being then only necessary till the commencement of fermentation, if it is advantageous to establish a free communication between it and the must, it is that garous substances which are formed during fermentation may escape easily, and mingle with, or dissolve themselves in it. It follows, also, from this principle, that when must is deposited in a close vessel, the carbonic acid, finding inseparable obstacles to its volatilization, is constrained to remain in the liquid, in which it is in part dissolved, and in making continual effort against it and its component parts, it slackens, and almost completely extinguishes the fermentation.

Thus, that the fermentation may establish itself, and follow out its periods in a prompt and regular manner, there must be a free communication between the fermenting mass, and the atmospheric air, which then serves as a vehicle for the principles disengaged in the process, and no obstacle is opposed to the swelling and subsiding of the mass.

If wine, fermented in close vessels, is frequently more generous and more agreeable to the taste, it is, because that part of the alcohol and aroma are retained, which in open fermentation is dissipated by the heat, and drawn out in a state of dissolution by the carbonic acid.

The free access of the air of the atmosphere hurries the fermentation, and occasions a great loss of the alcoholic and aromatic principles; while, on the other hand, the obstruction of this access slackens it, threatens explosion, or rupture balance the advantages with the disadvantages of each, keeping in view the circumstances in which he is placed.

The capacity of the vat, should also be varied according to the nature of the grape. When it is very ripe, or dried, and contains much saccharine matter, the must is thick and clammy, and the violence of a large mass fermenting, is necessary to decompose it. If it is not fully decomposed, the wine remains luscious and sweet, and does not acquire all the perfection it is susceptible of, till after being long in the cask.

On the other hand, when the grape has not attained a perfect maturity, when the temperature is cold, or when the vintage has been made when the grapes were wet, a large mass is advantageous on account of the heat it produces. All these causes, and their effects, should be continually present in the mind of the cultivator, because it is from them alone he can draw rules for his guidance.

Constituent Principles of the Must.

The saccharine principle. The sweet matter, the water, and the tartar, are the elements of the grape which appear most powerfully to influence fermentation.

It is not only to their existence that the first

cause of this sublime operation is owing, but it is to the very variable proportions between these different constituent principles, that the chief differences, presented by fermentation, are to be referred.

It appears proved, by the comparison of the nature of all substances which undergo the vinous fermentation, that only such as contain the saccharine principle, are susceptible of it; and it is beyond a doubt, that it is chiefly at the expense of this principle that alcohol is formed.

To give more precision to these ideas, it may be observed, that, at the present day, three sorts of sugar are distinguished, which, though very different in appearance, possess, in common, the property of yielding alcohol by fermentation.

The first species of sugar, is that extracted from the sugar cane, the red beet, the maple, and the chesnut, which is capable of being crystallized, and in these different plants is exactly of the same nature.

The second species of sugar, is afforded by the grape, by honey, &c. This has been reduced, by art, to the state of a fine powder, soluble in water, but all attempts to obtain it crystallized, have been unsuccessful. It is inodorous, agreeable to the taste, and its saccharine virtue is weaker than that of the first species, requiring three or four times the quantity to produce the same effect. An immense quantity of this kind of sugar was made in France, when the war almost shut up the sources which supplied the sugar of the cane.

The third species of sugar, is furnished by the juices of almost all fruits from which sweet extracts or syrups are made. This species of sugar, so abundant in the products of vegetation, is not susceptible of any other than its liquid form.

The existence of one or other of these kinds of sugar, is necessary for the production of alcohol by fermentation; and a natural consequence of this fundamental principle, which is confirmed by experience, is, that the bodies in which the saccharine matter is most abundant, should produce the most spirituous liquor. But the necessity cannot be too much insisted upon, of distinguishing between the sugar, properly so called, and the sweet principle. The sugar in the grape, from the decomposition of which, the alcohol results, is constantly mingled with a sweet substance, more or less abundant, and which serves for a ferment. It is a leaven, that, in almost all cases, accompanies sugar, but which, by itself, is not capable of yielding alcohol; whence it is, that rum is made from the produce of sugar-cane in its liquid state; sugar, separated by crystallization, if pure, being of itself not susceptible of fermentation.

M. Lequin distinguishes two sorts, or rather two varieties of leaven, the one soluble in water, the other insoluble. The former abounds in fruits, and forms the sweet principle of the grape; the other constitutes the yeast of beer. In the progress of fermentation, the first seems to pass into the state of the second. It separates itself from the fermenting body, and is precipitated, forming the lees and scum, which appear in a liquor under fermentation.

In the sequel, then, this sweet substance, or principle, shall be called the leaven; and it will be seen, when treating of fermentation, that it is sufficient to put this leaven, and the saccharine principle or sugar, in contact with water, to determine fermentation; and that, to the very variable proportions in which they are respectively present, in the grapes submitted to fermentation, the differences in the phenomena, and results of their decomposition must be referred.

This leaven is almost inseparable from the saccharine principle in the products of vegetation. They are found almost universally united, and more or less intimately combined.

They are present, then, in the grape, but in very different proportions. In some grapes, the saccharine principle predominates; in others, the leaven. In the former case, fermentation produces sweet and luscious wines, because the leaven is not in sufficient quantity to decompose all the sugar; in the latter, it fermentation is prolonged, the wines become sour, because the moment the sugar is decomposed, the leaven and the alcohol exert their action on the other principles; and develop the acid. In the former case, by the addition of leaven, the decomposition of the sugar may be continued, and a wine obtained which shall be spirituous, without being sweet, or in other words, shall be a *dry* wine. In the latter case, by the addition of sugar, the action of the leaven may be sustained, till it is all employed in the production of alcohol.

Grapes, though containing little saccharine principle, may nevertheless furnish a good wine; because the fermentation may develop a *bouquet*, which gives an agreeable taste.

In this case, it is necessary to arrest the fermentation, as soon as the small quantity of sugar is decomposed, and employ suitable means for preventing the action of the leaven on the other principles, in order to shun all ulterior degeneration or decomposition. This is practised in Burgundy, where, in some districts, the vinous fermentation is not allowed to act more than from twenty to thirty hours.

A grape may be very sweet and agreeable to the

taste, and nevertheless produce a very indifferent wine, because the saccharine principle may exist in very small quantity in a very sweet grape, and this is the reason that the sweetest grapes to the taste, do not always afford the strongest wines. The chapelas of Fontainbleau is a proof of this; it is one of the most delicious grapes to the taste, but at the same time, one of those which furnish a very bad wine.

The same sweet taste, or sweet principle, exists in many gums and mucilages, which contain no sugar; thus, it is most necessary to distinguish these two substances, on account of the difference of their effects. A little habit is sufficient for this, a palate accustomed to the really sugary grapes of warm climates, will not confound with them the grape, however sweet, in which a colder climate has not developed the saccharine principle.

The sugar, then, being considered as the principle, which, by its decomposition, gives place to the formation of alcohol, and the sweetish body, as the true yeast of the vinous fermentation; that the must may be susceptible of a good fermentation, it is necessary that it should contain these principles in suitable proportions.

A proper degree of fluidity in the must, is also one of the requisite conditions for procuring a good fermentation. It is as difficult to excite fermentation in a must too aqueous, as in one too thick. When the grape has attained a perfect maturity, the juice expressed from it is generally of the proper consistence, being in its mean term, when the grape has not been dried, between the eighth and fifteenth degree of the hydrometer of *Baumé* *

In general, the grapes of warmer, afford a thicker must than those of colder climates. During Chaptal's administration of the affairs of the interior, he collected in the nursery of the Chartreux, all the *species* and *varieties* of vines cultivated in France. After two years of culture, he found that the grapes of the south yielded a must thicker in consistence than those of the north; but, from the observations he made, he inferred, that they would degenerate by degrees, till they ceased to yield a juice similar to what they afforded in the dry and burning climates of Languedoc and Provence, and be assimilated in their qualities, to those which were cultivated in the same degree of latitude to which they had been removed.

---

* From the principle on which the hydrometer of Baumé is constructed, a must marking ten degrees on it, is of the same specific density as a hundred parts of fluid, consisting of ninety parts of water, and ten of sea salt, and so on in proportion. The ascending number on the scale, of course, indicates the increase of specific density in the fluid, and not the contrary, as in hydrometers for spirituous liquors, and fluids lighter than water.

It may be laid down as a principle, that, in cold climates, in humid soils, and when a rainy season has preceded the vintage, the grape contains more water and leaven than is requisite for the decomposition of the sugar formed in the fruit. In all these cases, the fermentation, when abandoned to itself, produces a wine with little spirit, weak, and diluted, and very subject to pass to acidity, or turn to ropiness, in consequence of the excess of leaven remaining, after the entire decomposition of the sugar.

These defects may be corrected or prevented:

1*st*, By pouring into the vat a portion of the must, which has been concentrated to one-third, or one-fourth, by boiling in a copper cauldron. The mixture in the vat should be agitated, till it is equally diffused, but care should be taken, not to thicken it to excess, for then the leaven is coagulated, and loses its power of promoting fermentation.

2*d*, By dissolving pounded or brown sugar in the must, in proportion as it is thinner than the due degree of consistence. Thus, if the must, expressed from grapes not perfectly ripe, marks the eighth degree of *Baumé*, while in years of perfect maturity, it reaches ten and a half, a quantity of sugar may be dissolved by heat in a cauldron of the must, and mixed in the vat, till the whole attains the consistence of 10½ degrees; the greater quantity of sugar being required, as the must is more diluted. It is necessary to employ pounded or brown sugar, because molasses fails in the desired effect. When mixed in the must of grapes, it remains in the mass without participating in its decomposition, or undergoing any alteration, although, when treated by itself, and properly diluted in water, it readily undergoes fermentation.

The thickening of the must by boiling, decides the fermentation, and makes it more regular and lively. The addition of sugar has the double advantage of augmenting the strength of the wine, and preventing the acid degeneration to which weak wines are subject.

In many wine districts, where they were forced to consume their wines within the first year, because the return of heat changed it to acid, the adoption of this process has given such durability to the wine, that it has been drank, a strong bodied wine, in its third and fourth year.

Chaptal was assured, by a rich magnate of Hungary, that by adopting these procedures, he had tripled the produce of his vineyards.

In districts where the wine does not keep, it is sufficient to bring it to the consistence of 10½ degrees by sugar. In seasons when the must is too aqueous, either on account of the grape not having attained its maturity, or the season having been rainy, the must should be brought to the degree of consistence which it possesses in seasons when it is perfectly ripe. In either of these cases, a strong bodied wine may be obtained, which will ameliorate with age, providing the fermentation is properly conducted.

By varying the proportion of sugar, the strength of the wine may be varied; and, though this process will not give that rich perfume which constitutes the chief excellence of some wines, it will not destroy what the imperfect maturity of the fruit may have developed.

Though the sugar of the cane, as being most in use, is usually employed, in some cases it may be economical to extract the sugar of the grape itself, in years of perfect maturity, to apply in less favourable seasons.

There are countries, where, to absorb the excess of humidity, quick-lime is mixed with the must, and the custom of drying the grapes before treading them, has the same end in view.

Another principle, contained by the juice of the ripe grape, is tartaric acid, which may be detected by the simple evaporation of that fluid; but verjuice, or the juice of unripe grapes, furnishes it in still greater quantity.

It appears, from the experiments of the Marquis

de Bullion, that the tartar, by facilitating fermentation, concurs, as well as the sugar, in augmenting the quantity of alcohol. By the addition of tartar and sugar, a much greater quantity of alcohol is obtained.

In 500 Paris pints (about 106 gallons) of must, to which 10 pounds* of brown sugar, and 4 pounds of cream of tartar was added, the fermentation was well established, and lasted 48 hours longer than in vats which contained the must without addition. Seven pieces of wine, in which sugar and tartar had been fermented in the above proportion, furnished 1½ piece of excellent brandy, while it required 12 pieces of wine, made without the addition, to yield one of brandy of the same strength.

Grapes containing much sugar, particularly require the addition of tartar, which should be added by boiling in part of the must; but, when the must contains tartar in excess, it may be enabled to furnish much ardent spirit by the addition of sugar.

It appears, then, that tartar facilitates fermentation, and concurs in rendering the decomposition of the sugar more complete. But cream of tartar

---

* The French pound is eight per cent. more than the English avoirdupoise.

should be added with much caution, and in very minute quantities.

SECTION II.

Of the Products of Fermentation.

Before entering upon a detail of the principal results afforded by fermentation, it may be advantageous, in a rapid manner, to trace its march through its various stages.

The commencement of fermentation is announced by the appearance of little bubbles of air at the surface of the must; by and by, they may be observed rising from the very centre of the mass, and bursting at the surface. Their passage across the liquid, agitates it throughout, and displaces all its particles, causing, very soon, a noise to be heard, similar to that produced by gentle boiling.

Small drops of the liquid may now be observed to rise from the surface, to the height of several inches. In this stage, the must is cloudy; every thing is mingled, confounded, and agitated; filaments, skins, flakes, stalks, and seeds, are swiming in all directions, and are elevated and precipitated through the mass, till they are finally fixed at the surface, or deposited at the bottom of the vat. It is in this manner, and in consequence of this intestine movement, that a crust, more or less thick, is formed at the surface, which is called the head of the vintage, *(chapeau de la vendange).*

By this rapid agitation, and by the continual disengagement of these aeriform bubbles, the must is considerably augmented in volume, and is raised above its former level in the vat. The bubbles, finding resistance to their volatilization, from the thickness or tenacity of the head, make their way through crevices, and cover their edges with scum. The heat, augmenting in proportion to the energy of fermentation, disengages, at length, an odour of alcohol, which spreads itself over the whole neighbourhood of the vat. The colour of the liquor turns gradually deeper, and in some cases, after many days, and in others, only as many hours, of tumultuous fermentation, the symptoms diminish, the mass subsides to its former bulk, the liquor becomes clear, and fermentation is almost terminated.

Among the most striking phenomena, and the most sensible effects of fermentation, there are four, which principally and peculiarly demand our attention, viz. the production of heat, the disengagement of gas, the formation of alcohol, and the colouring of the liquor. What observation has hitherto presented, respecting these phenomena, shall be considered under each respectively.

The Production of Heat.

It sometimes happens in cold countries, but particularly when the temperature is below the 54° of Fahrenheit, that the must deposited in the vat does not undergo any fermentation, if means are not resorted to, to heat the mass, such as introducing a portion of itself heated, agitating strongly the liquor, heating the surrounding atmosphere, covering the vat with cloths, &c. But immediately on fermentation commencing, the heat advances to intensity, and sometimes a few hours suffice to carry it to the highest degree; in general, it is in proportion to the swelling of the mass, and increases and decreases with it.

The heat is not always uniform throughout, it is frequently more intense towards the centre, especially in cases where fermentation is not sufficiently violent to confound and mingle all its parts. The head is, in this case, broken afresh, and agitated from the circumference to the centre, to establish, as far as possible, an equal temperature.

The following facts may be established as incontestable:—

1st, That at an equal temperature, the greater the mass submitted to fermentation, the greater will be the effervescence, the agitation, and the heat.

2d, That the effervescence, the agitation, and the heat, are greater when the skins, the stones, the stalks, &c. are allowed to ferment with the juice, than when the juice is submitted to fermentation, separated from these matters.

3d, That the fermentation may raise the heat from the 59° to the 86° of Fahrenheit, at least it has been seen in activity between these extremes.

4th, That the fermentation is so much the stronger, as the vats are well covered. Without the precaution is taken to cover the vats, the fermenting matter receives, every instant, the impression of the very variable temperature of the atmosphere, and the fermentation being weakened or excited, according to this variation, is necessarily imperfect. Besides, when the vat is open, there is a loss of alcohol, and the wine is weaker, and deprived of a portion of its perfume.

Of the Disengagement of Carbonic Acid.

The carbonic acid gas, which is disengaged from the must, and its deleterious effects, have been known as long as fermentation itself.

This gas, escaping in bubbles from all points, is elevated to the surface, where it displaces the air of the atmosphere, and occupies every where, the empty part of the vat, till it flows over the sides, and falls, by its weight, to the lowest part of the cellar.

It is to the formation of this gas, which carries off a portion of oxygen and carbon from the constituent parts of the must, that should be referred the principal changes occurring in fermentation; retained in the liquor, by every means which can be opposed to its evaporation, it contributes to preserve in it the aroma, and a portion of alcohol, which would exhale with it.

It is to this gas which brisk wines owe their property of frothing; being sealed up in glass before the fermentation is completed, the gas develops itself slowly, and remains compressed in the liquid, till the moment when relieved from compression by the removal of the cork, it escapes with force.

This acid gas gives to all liquors, impregnated with it, a tartish taste. Mineral waters owe to it their principal virtue; but it would give a very vague idea of its state in the wine, to compare its effects to those produced by its liberal dissolution in water.

The carbonic acid, which disengages itself from wine, holds, in solution, a considerable portion of alcohol. Chaptal believes himself to have been the first to demonstrate this fact, by shewing, that pure water exposed in vessels immediately above the fermenting must, was, after two or three days, impregnated with carbonic acid; and that it was sufficient to place the water, so impregnated, aside, in uncorked bottles, to procure a very good vinegar. At the same time that the vinegar is formed, flakes, of a nature very analogous to fibre, are abundantly precipitated.

The experiment sufficiently proves, that the carbonic acid carries off alcohol with it, and a small portion of leaven; and that these two principles, necessary to the formation of active acid, produce it when decomposed by the contact of the air. But another question arises, and one which can only be determined by experiment. Is the alcohol held in solution by the gas, or does it owe its volatilization only to the heat? It had been observed by Dom. Gentil, in 1779, that if a glass bell was turned down, above the must in fermentation, the interior walls were filled with a liquid, which had the odour and properties of the first phlegm which passes over in the distillation of wine; and M. Humboldt has proved, that if the froth of Champagne is received in bells, and these surrounded with ice, alcohol is precipitated by the simple impression of the cold.

It appears, then, that the alcohol is dissolved in the carbonic acid, and that it is to it that the vinous gas owes many of the properties which it possesses. Every one can perceive, by the effect of the froth of Champagne on the organs, how much that gaseous substance is modified, and is different from pure carbonic acid gas*.

It is not the most saccharine must which is generally employed in making brisk wines. If the fermentation of such were interrupted, by closing it in casks or bottles, to prevent the disengagement of the carbonic acid, the decomposition of the saccharine matter would also be prevented, and the wine would remain sweet, luscious, clammy, and disagreeable.

There are some wines, of which all the alcohol is dissolved in the garous principle; those of Champagne are an example.

---

* The word alcohol is employed above, although the substance referred to appears to differ from the alcohol extracted by distillation, as there is no term to express the vinous principle which exists in, and constitutes the character of wine; and which, dissolved in carbonic acid, as above, is a mixture of alcohol, aroma, and extractive. Although there is a strong analogy between the two substances, it is proper to notice the difference. The alcohol extracted by distillation is, in fact, the vinous principle separated from all the other principles which are united with it in the wine, and of all the elements which compose the wine, retaining only the hydrogen and the carbon. It is, with great propriety, called the spirit of wine.

It is difficult to obtain a wine at once red and frothy, because, to be coloured, it requires to be fermented with the husks; and this allows the escape of the gas.

There are wines which continue fermenting, slowly, through many months; and these, if put into bottles, at a proper time, become frothy. It is, in fact, this kind of wine which can acquire the property; those of which the fermentation is naturally violent, cease fermenting too promptly, and would burst the bottles in which it was endeavoured to close them.

The respiration of this gas is dangerous; all animals exposing themselves imprudently to its atmosphere, are suffocated; and these unhappy consequences are to be feared, when fermentation is conducted in a low place, or where the air is not renewed.

The garous fluid, displacing the air of the atmosphere, concludes by occupying all the interior of the cellar, and is the more dangerous that it is invisible. Its fatal effects cannot be too much guarded against; the place where fermentation is carried on, should never be entered without a lighted candle; as long as it burns, there is no danger, but when its light is obscured or extinguished, it is time to escape.

The dangers arising from it may be prevented,

by saturating it as it falls to the bottom of the cellar, by placing, in different parts, lime-water, or quick lime, and a place vitiated by it, may be disinfected by projecting on the floor and the walls, quick lime diluted with water. A caustic alkaline lie, such as that used by soap-makers, or ammoniac, will produce the same effects. The carbonic acid gas instantly combines with these matters, and the external air rushes in to supply its place.

Of the formation of Alcohol.

The saccharine principle, which forms one of the principal characters of the must, disappears during fermentation, and is replaced by alcohol, the essential characteristic of wine.

The way in which this phenomenon, or interesting train of decompositions and productions, may be accounted for, shall be considered afterwards. It is the object, at present, to point out the principal facts which accompany the formation of alcohol.

As the end, and the effect of fermentation, is the formation of alcohol, by the decomposition of the saccharine principle, it follows, that the formation of the one, is always in proportion to the destruction of the other; and that the alcohol in the wine will be abundant, in proportion to the abundance of saccharine principle in the must;

thus the alcohol may be augmented by the addition of the sugar, which may seem deficient in it.

It follows, from the same principles, that the nature of must, in fermentation, is modified and changed every instant. The odour, the taste, and all the other characters, vary from one moment to another; but, as the process of fermentation follows a regular march, all these changes may be traced, and presented as invariable signs of the different stages through which the must is passing:—1*st*, The must is distinguished by a peculiar sweetish odour. 2*d*, Its taste is more or less saccharine. 3*d*, It is thick, and its consistence varies as the grape has been more or less ripe, more or less saccharine. By the hydrometer of Baumé*, its consistence is between the 8th and 18th degree.

The grapes of warm climates yield a must which marks between 8° and 12°. Muscat grapes, and those from which wines of liqueur, (sweet wines) are made from 15° to 18°.

Scarcely has fermentation decidedly commenced, when all these characters are changed; the odour becomes less sweetish; the carbonic acid is abundantly disengaged, and being separated in the form of bubbles, rises to the surface, and forms a scum; the very saccharine taste gradually takes

---

* See the note, page 162.

a vinous character; the consistence diminishes; the liquor which hitherto was of an uniform appearance, is now distinguished by flakes floating through it, and these become gradually more insoluble*.

By degrees the saccharine taste is weakened, and the vinous taste gains strength; the liquor diminishes sensibly in consistence; the detached flakes become more isolated, and the odour of alcohol is distinguishable even at a distance.

In fine, the time arrives, when the saccharine principle does not make its presence evident to the senses; the taste and the smell indicate nothing but alcohol; the heat diminishes, and the fermenting mass subsides. The saccharine matter is, however, not altogether destroyed, a portion of it still remains, its existence being only masked by the alcohol which predominates, as has been determined by the very exact experiments of Dom. Gentil.

---

* These flakes are formed by the leaven which the heat and the fermentation precipitate from the liquid, where it was held in solution. In this state, it forms the lees of wine, and it is to separate it completely from the wine, that the different clarifications by isinglass and sulphur, are resorted to, with wines which it is wished to retain in the cask.

The interior decomposition of this substance takes place in consequence of tranquil fermentation in the cask.

Where fermentation has terminated all its periods, there exists no longer any sugar, the liquor has acquired a greater degree of fluidity, and only presents alcohol mingled with a little extractive and colouring principle.

Of the Colouring of the Vinous Liquor.

The juice which runs from the grapes, in their transport to the vat, ferments by itself, and yields *virgin* wine, which is not coloured.

Red grapes, when their juice is expressed by simple treading, furnish a slightly coloured wine*, provided they have not been too strongly pressed, or the juice has not been fermented on the husks.

The wine is more deeply coloured, as the must has fermented a longer time with the husks.

The wine is slightly coloured, in proportion as

---

* In Champagne, the white wines are made from white or red grapes, or from a mixture of both indifferently. It would seem, that the effect of a warmer climate, is to render the colouring matter more easily soluble. At Constantia, they make white wine only with white grapes. The proprietor of Great Constantia, with whom I conversed on the subject, seemed to consider the making of white wines with coloured grapes impossible.

the treading of the grapes in the vat has been slight.

The wine is more strongly coloured, as the grape is more ripe or less aqueous.

The liquor which runs from the husks, or grounds submitted to the press, is darker than that which runs from the grape by treading or slight pressing.

Although the fermentation develops a greater intensity of colour when the wine is generous, than when it is weak, there are grapes which furnish, naturally, more colouring principle than others, because their cuticle, or skin, contains more. Thus, the grapes on the borders of the Cher and Loire, in Touraine, are black, and yield wines so deeply coloured, that they are thick, and almost as black as ink, and are employed to colour white wines.

Such are the practical axioms sanctioned by long experience, from which result two fundamental truths:—The first, that the colouring principle of the wine exists in the cuticle of the grape;—the second, that though this principle may be extracted by a mechanical effort, it is not dissolved in the must submitted to fermentation, till the alcohol is developed in it.

From what has been said, it is easy for any person to assign a reason for all the procedures employed to obtain wine, more or less coloured, and to perceive, that it is in the power of the cultivator to have his wine of whatever colour he may desire.

SECTION III.

Of the Management of Fermentation.

FERMENTATION has no need of assistance or remedy, when the grape has attained its proper maturity, when the temperature of the atmosphere is not too low, and the must is in suitable quantity. But these conditions, without which, it is difficult to obtain good results, are not always united, and it is to art it belongs, to bring together favourable circumstances, and remove such as might operate disadvantageously in procuring a good fermentation.

The defects of fermentation deduce themselves naturally from the nature of the grapes subjected to it, and from the temperature of the air, which may be considered a most powerful auxiliary.

The must may be deficient in the quantity of saccharine principle necessary to the formation of a sufficient proportion of alcohol; and this defect may either result from the immaturity of the grape, from the sugar being too much diluted in water, or from the climate not developing a sufficient quantity of sugar in the grape. In all these cases, there are two ways of remedying the defect. The first is, by giving to the must the principle which it wants. A suitable addition of saccharine matter presents to fermentation the necessary materials for the formation of alcohol, and the defect of nature is thus supplied by art. This practice seems to have been known to the ancients, as they mingled honey, &c. with their wines before fermentation. But in our times, it has been proved by direct experiments, that it is possible, by the addition of sugar, to make a wine of good body, from the juice of unripe grapes, which, without such addition, would scarcely have undergone the vinous fermentation. The quantity of sugar to be added, must, of course, be determined by the quantity deficient; in general, from two to four ounces a gallon will suffice.

The other method, which is daily practised, is by boiling a quantity of the must in a cauldron, till it is concentrated to one-third, and pouring it into the vat. By this means, the aqueous part of the must is in some degree dissipated, and the fermentation proceeds with more force and regularity, and yields a more generous product. This process, almost always serviceable in cold climates, is requisite only in the warmer climates when the grape has not reached maturity, or when the season has been rainy. The same end may be attained, by drying the grapes in the sun, or in stoves, as is practised in some districts; and the custom of covering the walls of the vat with plaster has the same end, viz. the absorption of humidity in view.

A fault of an opposite nature, is by no means unfrequent; that is, the too thick consistence of the must, and the excess of saccharine principle. In this case, the fermentation is always slow and imperfect; the wine is sweet, luscious, and clammy; and it is not till after being long in bottle, that it loses these disagreeable qualities, and is only distinguished by its excellencies. This is the case with most of the white wines of Spain; but this kind of wine has its partizans, and, as has been several times observed, it is, in many places, the custom to concentrate the must, till it acquires the thickness of extract, by drying the grapes in the sun, or in stoves.

It would be easy, in all these cases, to promote the fermentation in must of too thick a consistence, by diluting it in water, by agitating the mass, or by applying artifical heat; but the application of these means, will, of course, be subordinate to the end in view, and will be varied by the experience the cultivator may have obtained of the quality of his grapes.

It should never be lost sight of, that the fermentation must be conducted conformably to the nature of the grape, and the quality of the wine it is desirable to procure. The grape of Burgundy cannot be treated like that of Languedoc. The merit of the one, consists in a perfume, which a strong and prolonged fermentation would dissipate; that of the other, in the quantity of alcohol, for the development of which, a long fermentation is necessary.

In cold countries, where the grape is always watery, and possessed of little saccharine principle, and in all countries after cold and humid seasons, the fermentation will be slow and difficult, but it may be accelerated and enlivened by various means:—

By evaporating a portion of the must, and pouring the remainder boiling into the vat; this is best accomplished by means of a funnel, which reaches within a few inches of the bottom, and which can be kept closed at the end, by means of a valve or bung, till it reaches the proper depth.

By stirring and agitating the liquor from time to time. This procedure has the advantage of re-establishing the fermentation, when it has ceased too soon, or slackened, and of rendering it uniform over the whole mas.

By covering the vat with cloths, by raising the temperature of the cellar, by means of stoves, and by introducing into the must heated cylinders, such as are employed for heating baths.

In some of the cantons of Champagne, when they make red wines, they accelerate and equalize the fermentation, by stirring the must, and breaking the head, which is weak and dispersed through the mass, by means of long poles with spikes attached to their extremities. This is called working the vat, and is a practice worthy of general imitation. In an experiment made on two vats, the contents of which were exactly of the same nature, and in every respect under the same circumstances, it was found that the one which was submitted to this operation, terminated its fermentation 12 or 15 hours before the other, which was left to itself, and that the wine was incomparably better in every respect.

By agitating the must, many good effects are produced; the heat, which is naturally greater in the centre, is more generally diffused, and the fermentation rendered more uniform.

By withdrawing the head from the action of the air, its ascescence is prevented, the scum is precipitated into, and mingled with the mass, and the yeast of which it is composed, is thus brought to act in nourishing the fermentation; and, on the whole, it is a process which cannot be too much recommended, especially in the fermentation of large masses.

It was the custom of the ancients, as appears from Pliny and others, to give peculiar qualities to wines, by the use of perfumes; and the most of the Greek wines owed their qualities to the plants, gums, and other substances with which they were perfumed. Now a days, it is generally considered, that these being only applied to mask a defect, or give a peculiar quality to the wine, are, generally speaking, uncalled for, from the superiority of modern wines, though it is still the custom, in some districts, to make use of the raspberry, and the dried flowers of the vine, for that purpose.

CHAPTER FOURTH.

Of the Time and Manner of discharging the Vat.

It has at all times been the particular study of agriculturists, to establish fixed signs, which should indicate the most favourable time for discharging the vat, and disposing of its contents in casks. Nor is this to be wondered at, for it is considered a point of great delicacy, and one on which much of the quality of the wine depends. But this, like other questions of a similar nature, has been too much generalized.

Some writers have endeavoured to fix a term for fermentation, as if its duration should not be varied *ad infinitum*, by many circumstances, such as the temperature of the air, the quality or maturity of the grape, the nature of the wine desired, the capacity of the vats, &c.

Accordingly, in different districts we find different signs pointed out, as indications of the best time for the operation. One of the most general of these, is the subsiding or sinking down of the head, which takes place when fermentation relaxes.

DISCHARGING THE VAT.

But almost all wines of colder climates, would be deprived of their most precious qualities, if this sign were waited for; and experience has proved, that far from degenerating, certain wines are improved, by remaining in the vat after fermentation has ceased.

In some countries, they judge of the completion of fermentation, by observing that the wine, when poured into a glass, shews no froth at the surface, or bubbles of air at the sides; or by agitating it in a bottle, to observe that no froth remains, or that it immediately disappears. But, besides that, the existence of scum, in almost all new wines, makes this an imperfect sign; effervescence is the most valuable property of some wines, and it is the chief study to preserve it.

In some places, they thrust a stick into the vat, and bringing it out quickly, examine if what runs from it into a glass, makes a circle of scum, *(fait la roue)*.

Others judge by the sweetish or spirituous smell of the wine brought out, by thrusting the hand into the vat, whether the time of discharging it has arrived. As soon as the sweetish taste or smell has given way to that of the wine, they proceed to the operation.

The disappearance of the heat is much trusted to by some cultivators; while others are guided by the colouring of the wine, allowing it to continue in the vat till it is sufficiently coloured. But the colouring matter depends upon the nature of the grape, and the must of the same soil and climate does not always shew the same disposition to colour, so this sign is therefore inconstant and insufficient.

Of late years, instruments, indicating the heat and consistence of the must, have been employed to ascertain the progress of fermentation, and fix the time for drawing off the wine; but it is understood, that their application has generally proved unsuccessful, from the same causes which make it impossible to lay down rules for this procedure.

It follows, that all these signs, considered separately, offer results which cannot be invariable, and that it is necessary to recur to the principles on which they depend, to form a judgment on this important point.

The chief end of fermentation being the decomposition of the saccharine principle, it would seem to follow, that it should be brisk or long, in proportion to the abundance of that principle. But two certain results of fermentation are the production of heat, and of carbonic acid gas; the tendency of the former, is to volatilize and dissipate the perfume or flavour, which gives the chief value to some wines; the latter, draws out with it, and causes the loss of a fluid, which, if retained in the liquor, would make it more *piquant* and agreeable. It is necessary, therefore, in weak, but agreeably perfumed wines, to arrest the fermentation at that point, which shall unite, in the most advantageous manner, the properties of spirituosity and perfume; and that the fermentation of brisk wines, should be conducted in such a way, as to preserve the carbonic acid, to which they owe their value, and, consequently, should scarcely be allowed to remain in the vat at all.

The most immediate product of fermentation is alcohol, it results immediately from the decomposition of the sugar; so, when the very sugary grapes of warm climates are submitted to fermentation, it ought to be brisk and prolonged, and particularly if the wine is destined for distillation, because then it is the object to procure the greatest possible quantity of alcohol. Without a long fermentation, the wine becomes luscious, and is not agreeable till it has been long kept.

In general, the grapes rich in saccharine principle require a strong and prolonged fermentation. On the other hand, grapes in which the saccharine principle does not abound, ought to ferment a shorter time, for the moment of the entire decomposition of the sugar, the leaven commences its action upon the remaining principles of the wine, and the formation of acetous acid is the result.

The most general rule, then, is to discharge the vat, when the sweet taste of the must has yielded to the sharp and frank taste of the wine. But it requires much experience to be able exactly to ascertain this point.

It is recommended, as soon as the fermentation has reached its maximum, to draw off, by a cock or spike-hole, a small quantity of the wine every two hours; by this means, the palate is habituated to distinguish the alterations in taste, and to recognise the first of the vinous impression. At first it will be sweetish, but the sweetness will gradually be lessoned, till it entirely yields to the vinous taste; after which, the vat should be immediately discharged.

From these principles, it is easy to judge, why in one country, the fermentation of a vat terminates in 24 hours, while in another, it is continued 12 or 15 days; why, one method cannot receive a general application, and why particular processes, when recommended to general practice, lead to error.

In the view of discharging the vat, another case engages the attention of the provident cultivator; this is, the preparation of his casks. This process is different, according to the end in view, with new or old casks. In the former, it is the object to extract, from the wood, the juices which would give an astringency and bitterness to the wine; in the latter, to clean from the cask the crust of tartar deposited by the wine it formerly contained.

For the new casks, the usual process is to wash them repeatedly with boiling and salt water, allowing these to remain long enough to penetrate, in some degree, the wood, and extract from it the hurtful principles; after which, they are completely drained off, and a pint or two of fermenting must is kept boiling, and skimmed, in readiness to pour in, and be agitated through the cask; warmed wine, or an infusion of the leaves and flowers of the peach, may be substituted for the must; the old casks are staved, and the tartar removed with a sharp instrument. They are then subjected to washing with must or wine, as in the former case, but sometimes water is made to suffice.

In Burgundy, the new wine is put into new casks, and after it is made; that is, after having undergone the different clarifications, it is put into old wood.

When the casks have contracted any bad quality, such as mouldiness, or taste of the woodbug, they must be burned in the way usually practised by coopers. It is possible to mask these defects, but their reappearance is to be dreaded.

The ancient Romans used plaster, with myrrh, and other perfumes, to saturate the interior of the casks, before drawing the wines from the vat. The Greeks added myrrh pounded with clay, with the double view of perfuming and clarifying the wine.

The casks being properly prepared, are arranged in parallel rows, in the cellar, and raised a few inches from the floor by means of frames. Some recommend, that they should be brought to the cock, and filled direct from the vat; while others consider the usual method of carrying the wine to them as preferable. Sometimes a hole is made in the head, and the wine pumped out by it, but the use of a cock or spigot, is in every point of view more advisable.

When all the wine which the vat can furnish is run off, there only remains the crust or head, and the grounds deposited on the bottom, on which the head has now also sunk down. The head is chiefly composed of the skins and stalks of the grapes; the deposit at the bottom contains, besides the husks or grounds, a quantity of leaven, which has been by the fermentation rendered insoluble. These residual matters are still impregnated with wine, of which a considerable quantity is extracted, by submitting them to the wine press; but as the head has generally contracted a little acidity, by being exposed to the atmospheric air, especially if the fermentation has been long continued, great care should be taken to separate it;

being pressed by itself, it furnishes an excellent vinegar; when the fermentation has been short, and it shews little signs of acidity, it is pressed with the rest.

The wine coming from the husks, submitted to the press, is generally mixed with what is already in the casks; the press is then opened, and the husks or marc is cut round with a sharp hatchet. What is cut from the edges, is then placed above and pressed anew; this is repeated for the third, and sometimes even for the fourth time.

The wine resulting from the first pressing, is the strongest, that of the last is more harsh and bitter, and more deeply coloured. The product of these different pressings is sometimes mingled, and put in different casks, to form a very deeply coloured and durable wine; and sometimes when it is desirable to add colour, strength, and a slight degree of astringency to the unpressed wine, and also to obtain one uniform produce of the vintage, the whole is mingled.

The marc thus strongly and repeatedly pressed, acquires almost the hardness of a stone; it is still of value, and is applied to various uses. In some countries it is distilled, and an inferior kind of brandy is made from it. This extract is of greater value, where the wine is generous, and the pressings less severe. In Burgundy, the marc being as little as possible exposed to the air, is put into casks, which are carefully closed, after a quantity of water has been added, which filtering through, is impregnated with the remaining wine; this is repeated till the water ceases to be affected, and the product forms a drink for the peasantry.

In the environs of Montpellier, the marc is pressed into casks, and carefully preserved for the manufacture of verdigris. In other places, it is exposed to the air, and, after being moistened with water, pressed for the vinegar it contains.

In many places, where food for cattle is scarce in the winter, it is preserved in casks, closed by a layer of clay, till winter, when, being moistened with water and mixed with bran, or other substances, it forms a mess of which horses and cows are remarkably fond.

CHAPTER FIFTH.

Of the Management of Wines in the Cask.

IN countries where the heat of the climate is sufficient to ensure the pretty constant maturity of the grape, and where, consequently, fermentation produces generous and very spirituous wines, there is nothing to fear from the acid degeneration; and the wine may, without danger, be kept in the vat, with the precaution, however, of covering it in such a way, as to prevent evaporation, and exclude, in a great degree, the contact of the air. In this state, the wine ameliorates, and is not discharged till it has deposited a great part of its impurities.

In countries where the grape is deficient in saccharine principle, and where fermentation has not power to destroy all the superabundant leaven, the vinous would soon be followed by the acetous fermentation, and it is necessary to discharge the vat, not only to withdraw the wine from the influence which the principles of degeneration exercise in a degree proportional to the quantity of the liquid, but because in the cask, it is more easily subjected to the necessary manipulations.

The notice of the particular processes of which wines in the cask are the subject, form the substance of the present chapter.

The wine deposited in the cask has not attained its last degree of elaboration, it is still troubled, and fermentation still continues; but, as the movements are now less violent, it is in this stage called the insensible fermentation.

For a short time after the wine has been put into the cask, a slight hissing or effervescing noise may be heard, which arises from the continued disengagement of bubbles of carbonic acid escaping at all points from the liquor. A scum is formed at the surface, which issues by the bunghole; and care is taken to keep the cask always full, that this disgorging of the wine may not be obstructed; a convenient method of allowing this, is to fix a leaf above the bung-hole.

In proportion as fermentation diminishes, the liquid subsides, and its subsiding is carefully watched, that the cask may be kept always full, by the addition of new wine. In some countries, the addition is made every day during the first month, every fourth day during the second, and every eighth day afterwards, till the wine is decanted. This is the way in which the delicious wines of Hermitage are treated:

In the cantons of Champagne, which produce red wines, when, towards the end of November, fermentation has ceased, advantage is taken of dry frosty weather to draw off and defecate the wines. Towards the middle of May, before the commencement of the heats of summer, it is again racked off, and this is called "drawing off clear." The casks are now fresh hooped, and deposited in the cellar. Before the wine is expedited to the consumer, or is bottled, it is decanted a third time, and clarified with white of eggs, in the proportion of six, diluted in a quart of water, to a cask containing about 200 bottles.

In general, the mountain wines of Champagne are bottled in November; but there are red wines, such as those of *Clos de Saint Thierry*, which are kept on the lees three or four years, in tuns containing from seven to ten casks each; by this they are wonderfully improved, but the same treatment, applied to any other than very strong wines, would inevitably cause their degeneration.

In Burgundy, as soon as the fermentation slackens in the cask, the bung-hole is closed, and a small hole pierced near; a small peg of wood which stops this. is occasionally removed to permit the escape of the remaining gas.

In the environs of Bordeaux, they commence to defecate the wine eight days after it is deposited in the cask. A month after, they apply the bung loosely at first, as it is removed every eight days to continue the process, but little by little it is fixed, without any risk being incurred. There, too, the white wines are drawn off towards the end of November, and defecated with sulphur; these require more care than red wines, because containing more lees, they are more subject to turn to ropiness. The red wines are not drawn off clear till the month of March. These are more susceptible of the acid degeneration than the white, and consequently require to be kept in cellars, during the heats of summer. It is the practice of some individuals, after the second decanting, to turn the casks, so that the bung may be at the side; it is thus hermetically sealed, and all contact with the external air, as well as loss, is prevented. It does not, in this case, receive the fining, or third drawing off, till it is about to be consumed.

The procedure is every where much the same as described above, and further details of the practice in other districts, would only lead to useless repetitions

When fermentation has altogether ceased, and the liquid is in a state of absolute rest, the wine is made; but it acquires new properties by the clarification, and it is by it that it is preserved from all danger of turning.

This clarification operates of itself, when the wine is in a state of rest; a deposit is gradually formed at the sides and bottom of the cask, which divests the wine of every thing there held in a state of solution or suspension. It is this deposit which is called the lees, and is a confused mixture of tartar, fibre, colouring matter, and in a great degree of that vegeto-animal principle which constitutes the ferment.

But these matters, although precipitated by the wine, and deposited in the cask, are still susceptible of being mingled with it by agitation, or by a change of temperature; and then, besides troubling and deteriorating the quality of the wine, they may cause a movement of fermentation, and turn it to vinegar. It is to obviate this evil, that the wine is decanted at different periods; that the greatest care is taken to separate from it the lees which it has precipitated; and that, by the simple means about to be described, every thing which it holds in a state of incomplete solution, is disengaged from it. By the aid of these operations, it is purged and purified, and divested of all those matters, which, by prolonging or renewing fermentation, might determine its acetification.

All that relates to the preservation of wines, may be reduced to the sulphuring, or defecation by means of sulphur; the decanting and the fining by isinglass.

SECTION I.

Of the Sulphuring of Wines.

This operation consists in the impregnation of the wine with a sulphureous vapour, and is performed by the combustion of sulphur matches.

These matches are differently composed; some employ the sulphur pure, and without any mixture, while others mix with it perfumes, such as the powder of cloves, cinnamon, ginger, the flowers of thyme, lavender, marjoram, &c. This mixture is melted over a moderate fire, in an earthen pan, and stripes of linen or cotton cloth are dipped in it, for burning in the casks. The ways in which these matches are used, are subject to the same varieties. Sometimes a match is suspended by an iron wire, within the cask about to be filled; after it is inflamed, the cask is closed, and it is suffered to burn till the atmospheric air is dilated and expelled with a hissing noise from the cask.

IN THE CASK—SULPHURING.

Two or three of these matches are sometimes burned in succession. When the combustion is finished, the acidity is almost removed from the interior of the cask, and the wine is then poured in.

In other countries, a different process is used; two or three buckets of wine are put into a good cask, a match is burned in it, as before described, and the wine agitated through it. After standing an hour or two, more wine is added, another match is burned, and the process is repeated till the cask is full. This method is practised at Bordeaux.

At Marseillan, near the city of Cette, in Languedoc, a kind of wine is made which serves to sulphur other wines. The must, as it runs from the grape, is taken before it has time to ferment, and a cask is one-fourth filled with it; a number of matches are burned above it, after which, the bung is put in, and the cask strongly agitated, till gas ceases to escape, when the bung is removed, and a new quantity of must added; matches are burned above, the cask is agitated as before, and the process is repeated till the cask is full. This must never undergoes fermentation, and is hence called *dumb wine;* it has a sweetish taste, and a strong smell of sulphur; it is mixed with other white wines, in the proportion of two or three bottles to a cask, and this mixture is equivalent to a sulphuring. At Bordeaux, and elsewhere, this wine is purchased, and employed in the defecation of the wines sold in England under the name of claret.

The sulphuring, at first, makes the wine muddy, and spoils its colour, but in a very short time it clears, and its colour is restored; but the colour of red wines is, generally, in some degree weakened by the process.

The advantage derived from it, is the prevention of the acid degeneration; the leaven, which was still held in solution by the liquor, being precipitated; and all ulterior fermentation prevented, provided the wine is, after some time of repose, decanted and fined. The sulphur also displaces the atmospheric air, whose contact is requisite to excite the actions of fermentation, and produces some particles of a very powerful acid, which opposes itself to the development of one more weak. Before the sulphuring takes place, the wine is drawn off, and all the lees previously deposited in the cask removed.

The ancients composed a mastich of pitch, one fiftieth of wax, a little salt, and incense, which they burned in the casks. This operation was designated by the term *picare dolia*, and the *vina picata*, (wines thus prepared) are spoken of by

Plutarch and Hippocrates. It was, perhaps, from this custom, that the juice was consecrated to Bacchus. In modern times, an agreeable perfume is sometimes given to weak red wines, by allowing them to remain above a bed of fir-tree shavings.

SECTION II.

Of the Decanting, or Racking off of Wines.

BESIDES the operation of sulphuring wine, there is another quite as essential. It consists, in the first instance, of decanting it, or drawing it off the lees, and afterwards of disengaging from it all the principles which are suspended, or feebly dissolved, that none may remain but those which are incorruptible.

The decanting should be, by Aristotle's advice, frequently repeated, *quoniam superveniente æstatis calore solent fæces subverti ac ita vina ascescere*.

In different wine countries, there are certain times of the year fixed for this operation, and these are, without doubt, established by centuries of observation and experience. In Burgundy and Hermitage, the periods are March and September. In Champagne, about the middle of October, the middle of February, and towards the end of March. It is always performed in dry and cold weather, as it is only during its continuance that the wine is in a state of rest. It is troubled, and made cloudy, by south winds and moist weather, it should not, therefore, be touched while they prevail.

Baccius has left us excellent precepts respecting the time for this operation; he recommends, that weak wines should be drawn off during the winter *solstice;* middling wines during the spring; and the most generous wines in summer. He lays it down as a general rule, that wines should never be drawn off, but when the north wind blows; and adds, that wine which has undergone this operation during the full moon, turns to vinegar.

The method of drawing off the wine should be determined with infinite precautions, and such as can only seem indifferent to those who are unacquainted with the effect the atmospheric air is capable of producing on this liquid. For example, if a hole is made, or a cock placed within three inches of the bottom of the cask, the wine running out determines a movement in the lees, and at the same time is in contact with the atmosphere in its progress; so that, from both of these causes, it may contract a disposition to acidity.

Part of these inconveniences are remedied by the use of a syphon, the movement caused by it being more gentle, and by its means the depth required may be penetrated to, without the lees being agitated.

But all the inconveniences of every other mode are avoided, by the aid of a sort of pump, the use of which is established in Champagne, and some other wine countries.

This consists of a leathern pipe, from four to six feet in length, and about two inches in diameter, terminated at both ends by wooden pipes, the diameter of which is diminished towards the extremities. The bung of the cask, about to be filled, being removed, one extremity of the pipe is introduced into the aperture, and firmly and closely fixed in it. A good cock is placed within from two to three inches of the bottom of the cask to be emptied, and to it the other extremity of the pipe is applied. When the cock is turned, one half of its contents will flow from the full to the empty cask, and the remainder is made to follow, by the following simple process: A pair of bellows about two feet in length, the handle included, and ten inches in width, is provided, a valve of leather is fixed at the end of the tube, which is then continued by the addition of a wooden pipe, to carry down the air.

This pipe is introduced into the bung-hole, and fixed there; when a blast of the bellows is given, whole in a vessel, they remove the scum which is formed at the surface; a small part of the wine is withdrawn from the cask, and is replaced by this composition. At the conclusion of three or four days, the wine clears, and becomes agreeable to the taste; it is allowed to settle eight days more, and is then drawn off

To restore a wine which has been clarified, but is again tainted with floating lees; two lbs. of flint calcined and pounded, is mixed with ten or twelve whites of eggs, and a good handful of salt; the whole is beat up with about two gallons of wine, which is poured into the cask.

These compositions vary *ad infinitum*, sometimes starch, rice, or milk, is made use of; and other substances more or less capable of enveloping the principles which make the wine turbid.

Wines are frequently clarified, and an unpleasant taste corrected, by digesting on chips or shaving of beach; these are prepared, by being stripped of their bark, boiled in water, and afterwards dried in the sun, or in a kiln. A quarter of a bushel of these chips is sufficient for a cask containing seventy gallons of wine, producing a slight fermentation, which clears it in twenty-four hours.

The art of mixing wines, so as to correct one by another, to give body to those which are weak, colour to those which need it, perfume to those which have none, or have one which is bad, cannot be described; it is always the taste, the eye, and the smell, which must be consulted; it is the very variable nature of the substances employed, which ought to be studied. It is sufficient to observe, that all which relates to this part of the manufacture of wines, may be reduced to the following:—

1st, To the sweetening of the wines, by the addition of concentrated must, honey, sugar, or of another very sweet wine.

2d, To the colouring of wines, by an infusion of turnsole cakes, the juice of the elder-berry, logwood, and more particularly of a black, and generally very rude wine, which is made for the exclusive purpose.

3d, To the perfuming of the wine, by the admixture of syrup of raspberry, an infusion of the flowers of the vine, which are suspended in the cask, as was the practice in Egypt, according to Hasselquist; and,

4th, To the mixing of brandy with the wine, to give that degree of strength, which the taste of numerous consumers requires.

In Orleanois, and elsewhere, a wine is made which is called rasped wine, *(vin râpé).* It is made, by pressing picked grapes in wine; or by charging the wine press with a layer of grapes, and a layer of vine shoots alternately; or by infusing the shoots in wine. In either of these cases, the preparation of the wine is completed, by strongly boiling; after which, it is used for giving strength and colour to the weak and ill coloured wines of cold and humid countries.

Although the wine may ferment at any time, there are certain seasons of the year, in which it seems peculiarly liable to a renewal of fermentation. These are, when the vine begins to shoot, when it is in flower, and when the grapes are colouring. At these critical periods, it is necessary to watch the wine with much care; and, when the movements of fermentation commence, they can only be prevented by the processes above described. These are also the seasons which should be taken advantage of, to mix the wines with each other.

The following observations on this branch of the subject, are from an excellent and comprehensive article on wine, by Dr. M'Culloch, in the supplement to the Encyclopedia Britannica:—

The mode of performing this operation, which requires great experience and judgment, is to select, first, that period of the year in which the wines shew a disposition to renew their fermentation, which is in the spring. They are then said, in English, to bear the *fret;* and hence the operation is called fretting-in. It is only thus, that a new and fine wine can be produced. The operation of mixing different wines, in all cases, disturbs both, so that they become foul; they also tend to ferment again, till a new balance of all their principles is produced; and thus it is expedient, to accelerate and determine this fermentation, so as to form a proper compound, without which, the new wine would be perishable. After this, also, it becomes necessary once more to have recourse to sulphuring, fining, and racking; and not till all this has been gone through, is the wine completed. In the Bourdeaux practice of mixing clarets, the must, or sulphured wine, is sometimes added at the same time, where the wines, being of very discordant qualities, a dangerous fermentation might be excited.

In the wine countries, it is usual to cultivate particular grapes or wines, rough, or coloured, or astringent, or high flavoured, for the mere purpose of mixing with others; so far is this art from being so simple, as is commonly imagined.

In the district Medoc, the seat of the better claret wines, there are, besides the third and fourth classes, six or eight kinds of wine, known by the names of *gros bourgeois, petit bourgeois, artizan,* and *paysan;* and these are manufactured with others, for the English and Irish markets chiefly, by means of Spanish wines, by mixing with the strong wines of Benecasto and Alicant. The same is true of the Grave wines.

This is the great mixture, in fact, by which the market is filled, to almost any extent, with claret wines, so called; and these mixed wines are almost the only ones we drink in this country. If that be a fraud, it must be remembered, also, that such is British taste in wine, and that claret is in general esteemed here, only in proportion to its strength. Of the stronger and finer wines, there is even not enough for our consumption. Strength is obtained, however, by some of the south of France wines also.

The French wines, of which we have been speaking, will not endure to be rendered stronger by means of brandy. The property of this substance, thus mixed, is to decompose the wine in process of time, causing the extractive matter, or mucilage, to be deposited, as well as the colour, as is daily seen in port wines, and thus diminishing their powers of duration. At the same time, it destroys their lightness and flavour, that peculiar indefinable delicacy, well known to drinkers of good wine, but quite imperceptible to British drinkers of port. In a certain sense, we may consider, that it is only the bad wines which will bear this medicine—those which have no flavour of their own, and whose whole merit already is their strength. What sort of a compound is made of a weak wine with brandy, ought to be known to those who drink what is called Lisbon wine; but a depraved taste has rendered it necessary to our nation, and thus it is largely used, even in those wines of Portugal and Spain, of which the chief fault is that of being too strong already. We may thank the *Methuen Treaty*, for being condemned to drink, what Mr. Pinkerton calls, wine fit for hogs only. This mixture is performed in the same manner, at the period of fretting; and the proportion is regulated, partly by the taste of the consumers, and partly by the badness of the wine. As it must have a certain strength, the worst wines require most; and hence, whenever we taste the brandy in wine, we may be sure it is bad. It is a taste sufficiently perceptible to those who know what real wine is.

Many wines have so little flavour naturally, that they can scarcely be considered to possess any. There are few, indeed, that possess this quality in any great degree; and, of these flavours, a large proportion is bad. Wines so highly perfumed by nature, as Hermitage and Burgundy, are rare; indeed, these are almost the only examples, and after them, we may consider the finest clarets, and then the finest of the Rhine wines. The sweet wines which possess it, are well known; and these, also, are but a small part of the total number in this class, being almost limited to Paxaret, and the Muscat wines, among which Rivesaltes stands first. Constantia has rather a taste than a flavour, and what the ordinary sweet Spanish wines possess, is rather bad than good; though, like the taste of sherry, and porter, and olives, they may become agreeable by habit.

In Britain, our chivalrous and baronial ancestors, perfumed their wines with every strange ingredient that can be imagined; but that was the age of spicery and perfumes; and he who eats cinnamon with his pork, might drink ambergrease with his wine. The flavour of Madeira is nothing but that which we know, is given by means of bitter almonds, and, we believe, of sweet almonds also; and the same practice is followed for the wines of Saint Lucar. That which is called the *borrachio* taste in wine, is, for the most part, that of the tar with which the seams are secured. In sherry, the flavour seems to be produced by the destruction of the acid, the consequence of the lime used,* and possibly by some other action of that substance on the fruit. One of the most common ingredients used for flavouring wines, is oak chips; and from this, the wretched Lisbon wines acquire the little taste they have. Orris root is also a common ingredient, and the high-flavoured wine of Johannesberg, is imitated by a proportion of rose water. The orris root gives a very agreeable flavour, and is used in France; and there, also, it is the custom to use raspberries, and other highly perfumed fruits. A very agreeable flavour is also said to be produced by wormwood. The flowers of the vine itself are also used for the same purpose, their smell much resembling that of our mignonette. This last is an ancient practice in Egypt.

---

* In making sherry, the grapes are first slightly dried, and then sprinkled with quicklime. They are then wetted with brandy when introduced into the press, and a further portion is again added to the must before fermentation. It is highly probable, that, by this practice, the brandy is more perfectly combined in the wine, and the fluid rendered more uniform than in Port and Madeira wines, to which it is not added, till the insensible fermentation, or indeed, in the case of Madeira, till the wine has been racked three months after having been made. The remainder of the practice for sherry, consists in racking repeatedly, at intervals of a month or two, fresh brandy, in small quantities, being added at each stage of the process.

The method of gaining this end, requires some delicacy and attention, in particular, care is taken that it be not overdone. As the full fermentation would destroy the more volatile flavours, these substances are only introduced towards its decline. In Madeira, the nut-cake is put into the cask; flowers are suspended in a net, or cloth, either in the fluid or the vacant part of the cask, and thus a small quantity of raspberries communicate a very considerable flavour.

SECTION V.

Of Vessels proper for containing Wines.

WHEN wines are completely clarified, they are kept in casks or bottles; the largest and best closed vessels are the best. Every one has heard of the enormous tuns* of Heidleberg, in which the wine is kept to ameliorate, and in which, it is said to keep for centuries without degenerating. In the south of France, tuns of very great capacity

---

* One of these is said to contain 58080 gallons, and the wine is said to be a hundred years old. Strangers are, with much ceremony, made to taste it, in a superb cup called *wiederkom*. The quantity drawn out, is annually replaced by new wine.—*Topograpie de Vignobles*, p. 415.

(called *foudres*), are also employed. They are constructed of oak staves, several inches in thickness, encircled with strong iron hoops, and carefully varnished on the outside.

The Romans drew off the wine from the cask, to bestow it in earthen vessels, called amphora and cada. The amphora was of a square form, and had two handles; the cada was in the form of a pine-apple; they were both varnished within, and terminated by straight necks, which were closed with pitch and plaster. The more generous wines, were exposed to the open air, in well closed vessels; the more weak, were kept under cover. Galen observes, that, after the wine was put in bottles, it was exposed to a strong heat, in a close chamber, and afterwards to the sun's rays on the house-top, to make it ripen sooner.

In order that wine may be preserved and ameliorated by keeping, the choice of vessels, and the place to bestow them, are by no means matters of indifference. Glass certainly deserves the preference, not only because it contains no principle soluble in the wine, but because bottles can be easily packed, and withdrawn from the contact of the air, from humidity, and from the variations of the atmosphere. They should be carefully corked and sealed with wax, or have their necks plunged into melted wax. Some put a little oil above the wine, in the neck of the bottle.

Casks are, however, the vessels most commonly in use; they are generally constructed of oak, and of various dimensions. Their great inconveniences are, their containing substances more or less soluble in the wine; their being easily affected by variations of the atmosphere; and their allowing an easy passage to the ingress, or egress of air.

Earthen vessels would have the advantage of keeping a more equal temperature, but they are all more or less porous, and, at the long run, the wine is altered. Vessels of this description, were found in the ruins of Herculaneum, in which the wine was quite dried up; and one of a similar nature, and in the same state, was dug up on the site of Pompey's palace in Dauphiny.

The Romans remedied the porosity of their earthen vessels, by imbuing them with wax within, and with pitch without; the whole external surface was then carefully enveloped in waxed cloths. Pliny condemns the use of wax, because, according to him, it caused the ascescence of the wine.

Whatever may be the nature of the vessels used to contain the wine, it is necessary to choose a vault or cellar, which, by its situation, is removed from circumstances injurious to it:—

1st. The exposure of a vault ought always to be towards the north; its temperature is then less variable than when it opens towards the south.

2d. It ought to be of sufficient depth, to preserve always the same temperature.

3d. There ought to be a constant, though not excessive degree of humidity. An excess of moisture determines the mouldiness of paper, bungs, casks, &c. The contrary extreme dries the casks, and allows the wine to transude.

4th, There ought to be a very small degree of light; an excess of light acts like dryness, and darkness like moisture.

5th, The vault ought to be removed from joltings or shakings. Brisk agitations, and those lighter tremblings, caused by the passage of vehicles, stir the lees, mingle it with the wine, and induce its acetification; thunder produces the same effect.

6th, All green wood, vinegar, and all matters susceptible of fermentation, ought to be removed from the vault.

7th, The reflection of the sun's rays, which, in varying the temperature, alters the properties of the wine, ought also to be shunned.

According to these principles, a wine vault ought to be sunk some feet under ground, its openings should be directed towards the north, it should be distant from streets, roads, workshops, common sewers, currents of water, &c. and should be roofed by an arch.

CHAPTER SIXTH.

Of the Degenerations and Spontaneous Alterations of Wine.

FOR the better understanding of the degenerations to which wines are subject, it may be advantageous to recur to some of the principles already developed in the preceding chapters.

The vinous fermentation, being the effect of a reciprocal action between the saccharine principle and the leaven, or vegeto-animal principle, must afford, when terminated, one of three results:—

1*st*, If the two principles of fermentation are found to exist in the must, in suitable proportions, they will be entirely decomposed by each other, and neither sugar nor leaven will remain after fermentation has ceased. In this case, there are no grounds to fear any ulterior degeneration, because the wine does not contain any germ of decomposition.

2*d*, If the saccharine principle predominates over the leaven in the must, this latter will be all employed in decomposing a part of the saccharine principle, and the wine will necessarily retain a taste of sugar, more or less decided. In this case, also, there is no danger of the wine turning to acidity, or ropiness, because these effects are produced by an excess of leaven. Wines of this description, may be kept any length of time which may be desired, and will improve by keeping, inasmuch as the saccharine taste disappears, by the gradual combination of the sugar with other principles, or by its being converted by the insensible fermentation into alcohol.

3d, But if the leaven predominates over the saccharine principle, a part of this leaven is sufficient for the decomposition of all the saccharine principles, and that which remains, is the cause of almost all the maladies incident to wines; in fact, this principle of fermentation existing in the wine, either re-acts upon the principles contained in it, and produces the acid degeneration; or, by disengaging itself from the liquid by which it was held in solution, causes that sirupy consistence, which produces the phenomenon called grease, or ropiness.

It is clear, that the defect, in these two most general results of fermentation, may be corrected, by supplying to the mass a portion of that principle, which may be necessary to establish a just proportion between the principles of fermentation. Where the sugar predominates, leaven may be supplied; and when it is the leaven which is in excess, as is the case in all weak wines, the produce of immature grapes, or of those which naturally contain little saccharine principle, sugar may be added.

By adhering to these principles, a complete and entire fermentation may always be procured, and wine may be made, which shall incur little danger of alteration; but, by this means, we would be deprived of many excellent wines, which owe their excellencies to fermentation, incomplete, but conducted with the view of developing the most precious qualities, such as perfume in the wine.

To these principles, it is easy to refer every thing which experience teaches us relative to the maladies of wines.

Almost all wines ameliorate by age, and cannot be regarded as having attained their perfection, till a long time after they are made. This is peculiarly the case with luscious or sweet wines, but delicate wines turn to grease or to acidity, with such facility, that, to preserve them for several years, requires the greatest precautions.

There is no vineyard, the wine of which, has not a fixed and ascertained duration. This duration varies in the wine of the same vineyard, according to the weather which has prevailed in the season, at the time employed in the fermentation.

When the season has been wet or cold, when the grape has not ripened perfectly, or is filled with water, the wine is weak, and of little durability.

In general, grapes coming from rich soils, and those which are the produce of too young, or newly propagated vines, yield wines which do not keep. Fine and delicate wines are also very difficult of conservation.

The ancients, as we are informed by Galen and Atheneus, had determined the epoch of ripeness, or the age at which their principle wines ought to be drunk; *falernum* was fit for use from its 10th to its 20th year, after that period, it became too heady; *albanum*, of which there were two kinds, one sweet, the other dry, at its 15th year; *surrentinum* was so luscious and clammy, that it only began to be of use at its 25th year; *tiburtinum* was light, and easily changed; it was used from its 10th year, &c.

The cares bestowed in decanting, in clarifying, and in fining wines, contribute most powerfully to their conservation; and these cares should be redoubled, when they are intended to pass the seas, as it is only to the repetition and multiplication of these operations, that we owe the power of transporting wines to all climates, without fear of their degeneration.

Among the maladies to which wines are subject,

the most frequent and the most dangerous, are the turning to ropiness, or grease, and the turning to acidity. Most other alterations are attributable to neglect, in not preparing and cleaning the vessels in which they are bestowed, or to carelessness, or ignorance, in conducting the different operations.

SECTION I.

Of that malady of Wine called Grease, or Ropiness.

This is an alteration which wines frequently undergo, losing their natural fluidity, and thickening into an oily or sirupy consistence.

Very generous wines, of which the must contained much sugar, never turn to ropiness, if they have undergone a good and sufficient fermentation. It is only delicate wines, and wines which are poor in alcohol, that are subject to it. Weak wines which have fermented very little, are most subject to this malady, and the more so, if they are made with grapes freed from the stalks.

Wines turn to ropiness in the best closed bottles, but rarely in the cask; of this truth, they are well convinced in Champagne, and Burgundy, where sometimes a whole vintage contracts this alteration.

Ropy wines furnish, by distillation, a very small quantity of spirit, which is greasy, coloured, and of a bad quality.

Wine attacked with this malady, is flat, insipid, and indigestible; it contracts a yellow colour, and, when poured out, drops in threads like sirup.

Wines are discovered to have contracted this malady, when they discolour, or turn yellow.

In the wines of Champagne, a white or yellow sediment is the worst; the presence of this sediment alone announces, that the wine has turned to ropiness.

To understand properly the determining cause of this malady, it is necessary to set out from the following facts, which are established by experience.

Wines which turn most easily to ropiness, are,

1*st*, The wines least charged with alcohol.

2*d*, Weak wines which have fermented without the stalks; and,

3*d*. White wines bottled before they have undergone all the periods of fermentation.

To conceive this degeneration, it is again necessary to recur to the principles developed in treating of fermentation. It was there observed, that the two principles of fermentation, are sugar, and a leaven which is analogous in its nature to animal gluten; and that, to procure a perfect fermentation, a certain proportion between these principles was necessary. When the sugar predominates, the wine remains luscious and sweet; when the leaven is in excess, there remains, after fermentation, a greater or less quantity of this matter in a state of semi decomposition, imperfectly dissolved in the wine, and disengaging itself with ease; this is the substance which causes ropiness in weak wines.

When the fermentation has completed all its stages, and has entirely ceased in the cask, the gluten has become perfectly decomposed; it has passed almost to the state of fibre, and has become insoluble: at first, it swims in the wine, in the state of filaments, and concludes, by depositing itself and forming the lees. The wine may be entirely freed from it, and all degeneration prevented, by the processes of sulphuring, fining, and decanting.

It has been observed, that wine produced from very ripe, and consequently very sugary grapes, is not always exempt from this malady; but in this case, it must be attributed to the precipitation with which it has been bottled, the fermentation being suspended, the two principles, already altered in their nature, are become less soluble, and can disengage themselves from the liquid. Sugar, gum, and oil, only differ in a small degree, in possessing a little more or less of oxygen, carbon, and hydrogen, and the transformation of these substances into each other, is of daily occurrence in the operations of nature.

When there is reason to dread the appearance of this malady in the wine, the following means of prevention may be resorted to :—

1*st*, To dissolve sugar in the must, when it is weak and watery.

2*d*, To leave part of the stalks to ferment with the must.

3*d*, To allow the fermentation to be completed in the cask ; and,

4*th*, To decant the wine into another sulphured cask, and to clarify and fine before bottling it.

If, in spite of these precautions, the wine turns to ropiness in the bottles, it is necessary to empty them into a cask, and have recourse to the following procedure :—

For a barrel, containing from 70 to 80 gallons, take about a gallon of good wine, in which, after bringing it to the boiling point, dissolve from 8 to 12 ounces of pulverized cream of tartar, and as much sugar. When these two substances are well dissolved, pour the whole into the cask containing the ropy wine. The bung-hole must then be closed, and a small hole which is made beside it, also closed with a peg; this done, the cask must

be violently rolled and agitated, for five or six
minutes, and restored to its place, the bung being
placed undermost. If, during the operation, there
is reason to fear an explosion from the efforts of
the gas, the peg may be removed for a moment,
and immediately returned. After two days of
repose, the wine must be fined in the usual manner. The bung being strongly fixed, after remaining five or six days more, it will become clear,
and quite free from ropiness. It should then be
drawn off with care, and separated from the lees.
This process, which was first proposed in France,
by M. Herpin, is every where practised with great
success.

The numerous methods which have been successively employed for the cure of this malady,
have all for their object, either to re-establish
fermentation, or to precipitate the ropy principle.
In the former case, they have employed dried
grapes, the lees of new wine, sugar-candy, diluted
flower of wheat, exposure to a high temperature,
&c. In the latter, the processes of sulphuring and
fining, chips of beech, alum, pounded flint, &c.
When the degeneration is not complete, it frequently happens, that the wine re-establishes
itself, in the next, or second spring following,
when the greasy milky sediment, which was at the
bottom of the cask, becomes brown, dries, and

and forms itself into scales, and the wine recovering its transparency, is pronounced cured.

It has been observed in Champagne, that if, in the quantity of grapes employed in making white wine, the white have prevailed over the black, a yellowness mingles itself with the ropiness, and the wine is no longer saleable. It has a flat and insipid taste, and a colour of copper, and can only be employed in mixing with common red wines, which have a deep colour, and a harsh taste.

An effect analogous to ropiness, is frequently observed in beer, in the decoction of nut-galls, and in many other vegetable preparations.

SECTION II.

Of the Spontaneous Ascescence of Wine.

As the ascescence of wine is by far the most common, one might almost say it is the most natural disease of wine; for the vinous is naturally followed by the acetous fermentation. But the causes which produce, and the phenomena which announce and accompany it, being known, it is easy to employ means for its prevention.

The ancients admitted three principal causes of

the acetification of wines, viz. the wateriness of the wine, the inconstancy of the weather, and agitations.

It has been observed, in the course of this chapter, that, when the saccharine principle predominates over, or is in just proportion with the leaven, there is no risk of acetous fermentation, provided the usual processes of clarifying, decanting, &c. have not been neglected; but, when an excess of leaven remains, after the decomposition of all the saccharine matter, it acts upon the other principles of the wine, and, combining with the oxygen of the atmospheric air, causes the liquid to pass to the acid degeneration; and this result is only to be avoided, by the application of the several processes already described, for divesting the wine of all the remaining leaven, or by mixing with it sugar, or a very sugary must, to continue the vinous fermentation, and employ all the excess of leaven in the production of alcohol.

This doctrine, as shall be seen, is confirmed by observation:—

1*st*, Wines never turn sour till the vinous fermentation has terminated; or, in other words, till the saccharine principle is completely decomposed; and hence the advantage of putting the wine into the cask, before all that principle has disappeared. The fermentation thus continued and prolonged, removes the causes of the acetous decomposition; hence, also, the custom of adding sugar or must to the cask, when fermentation has ceased, and there is reason to dread the commencement of acidity.

2d, The least spirituous wines, are those which turn most quickly. It is necessary to distinguish carefully the alteration of weak wines, and of those of a more generous description; in the former, the principle of fermentation separates itself, and remains dispersed in the liquor, which it renders muddy; the colour becomes lees of wine, but the taste is scarcely acid. This decomposition is called troubling, or turning. In the latter, as the alcohol is more abundant, the phenomena are also different, and the acid becomes more strong. The difference between weak and very generous wines, is this, that these latter never turn to acid, when, by the usual processes of clarification, &c. they have been divested of the principle of fermentation, while the latter always contains enough of that principle, inherent in them, to cause their ascescence.

3d, Some very old, well prepared, and very generous Languedoc wine, did not lose its qualities when exposed, in uncorked bottles, to the heat of the sun, during forty days in July and August;

It is most probable that the acetification comonly the colouring principle was always precipitated in form of a membrane, which covered the bottom of the bottle.

It is to be observed, that this wine took a slight bitterness, and disengaged some filaments of lees, that formed a cloud in the liquor, and which confirms the theory about to be developed, on the bitterness which some wines acquire, when of a great age.

4th, The wine does not turn sour without the contact of the air; the atmospheric air mingled in the wine, is a real acid leaven.

When the wine frets, *(pousse)* it allows the gas it contains to escape, or exhale. Rozier has proposed to adapt a bladder, to a pipe fixed at the top of the cask, to judge of the absorption of air, and the disengagement of gas; when the bladder fills, the wine tends to fret; when it empties, it turns to acidity.

When the wine frets, the cask allows the wine to ooze through; and if a gimlet hole is made, the wine escapes with hissing and froth. When, on the contrary, the wine tends to acidity, the staves of the cask and the bung are dry, and the air rushes in as soon as the bung is removed.[*]

---

[*] The fretting of the wine has all the characters of a second fermentation. The ascescence, is a degeneration of the vinous

It may be concluded, from this principle, that wine kept in perfectly closed vessels, is not susceptible of acetification.

In countries where wine is of great value, and consequently heavy losses are sustained by its acetification, it has been observed, that the acidity manifests itself, at first, in the highest part of the cask, whence it descends gradually through the whole mass; taking advantage of this circumstance, they have been induced to draw off the liquor from beneath; and, by this very simple process, to save a great part of the wine in which degeneration had commenced.

It is most probable, that the acetification commenced in the superior layers of the wine, or those next the bung, merely because it was more penetrable to the air.

5*th*, There are times of the year in which wine is more liable to the acid degeneration. The periods are, the return of hot weather, the commencement of the motion of the sap in the vine, the time of its flowering, and of the colouring of the grapes. It is peculiarly necessary, at these times, to guard against it. A change of temperature has also a tendency to induce the acetification

---

liquor, and is only excited by the contact and absorption of the oxygen of the atmospheric air.

of wine, especially if the temperature is elevated; if it rises to between 70° and 80° of Farenheit, its degeneration is rapid, and almost inevitable.

It is easy to prevent the degeneration, by removing all the causes assigned for it, but it is considered impossible to cause a retrograde march in the wine, when its acetification has decidedly commenced, though it is possible to mask its taste, by methods which are every where known—such as the following:—

By dissolving concentrated must, honey, or liquorice, in the wine, where the acidity has manifested itself; by this means, not only is the sour taste corrected, being replaced by the sweet taste of these ingredients, but by supplying saccharine principle to the leaven remaining in the wine, the vinous fermentation is renewed, and alcohol, in place of acid, is produced.

Wine is freed from the acid which may have been formed by the use of ashes, alkalies, chalk, lime, and even litharge, or vitrified lead, though the employment of this last substance, which forms a very sweet salt with acetic acid, is very dangerous. This criminal adulteration may be detected, by pouring some hydro sulphuret of potash into the wine, when an abundant black precipitate is disengaged.

The writings of those who have treated of the

subject, are full of receipts for correcting the acidity of wines.

Bidet affirms, that one-fiftieth of its bulk of skimmed milk, added to sour wine, re-establishes it, and that it may be drawn off in five days.

In this case, the milk only acts by removing the vegeto-animal principle, which is the cause of the acid degeneration. Others take four ounces of wheat, of the best quality, which they boil till it bursts; when cold, it is tied in a small bag, and plunged into the cask, where it is well stirred through with a stick. The seeds of the leek, of fennel, and many other substances, are also employed for the same purpose.

Besides the alterations above treated of, there are others, which, though less common, and less dangerous, are still worthy of notice.

Wine sometimes contracts a mustiness, which is commonly called, "taste of the cask," and may arise from two causes: either from the cask containing the wine having been tainted, worm-eaten, or decayed; or from lees of wine having been allowed to harden on it, even though the precaution had been used, of scraping it off before the wine was poured in; lime water, carbonic acid, and oxymuriatic acid gas, have been severally proposed, to remove from the cask the property of producing this defect. Others recommend, after carefully clarifying and decanting the wine, to infuse in it, for two or three days, a quantity of roasted wheat.

In Burgundy, when wine has contracted a " taste of the cask," it is passed over the lees of untainted wine, over which it is violently rolled, and when the musty taste has disappeared, it is carefully clarified. If the first operation does not succeed, it is repeated.

Another defect to which wines are subject, and which they acquire with age, is bitterness. Burgundy wines are peculiarly subject to it.

This is considered by Chaptal, as a continuation of their natural working in the glass, or in the cask; for wines divest themselves gradually, of their vegeto-animal principle, or leaven, which is deposited in the form of lees, decomposed by the insensible fermentation, or is precipitated by the sulphur, and extracted by whites of eggs, &c.

But when the wine is entirely divested of it, then the bitter principle, which is inherent in Burgundy wines, and which was only masked by the sweetness of the leaven, is evident in all its characters. What appears to prove this opinion, is that the wine keeps well, that it only acquires the defect by age, and that it does not free itself from it.

This defect may be corrected, by rolling the wine in the first lees discharged by another wine, or by adding a little dissolved sugar, or better still, by a pint of " dumb wine" (unfermented and sulphured wine) to each cask.

A phenomenon which has as much astonished, as embarassed those who have treated of the maladies of wine, is what is called *flowers of wine*. They are formed in the cask, but more particularly in the bottle, of which they occupy the neck, announcing, and constantly preceding the acid degeneration. This substance, which Chaptal at first considered a precipitate of tartar, was reduced to almost nothing by desiccation, and an analysis contained only hydrogen in very small, and carbon in very large proportion, appearing to be only a slight alteration of the vegeto-animal principle, which, as has been already observed, passes to the state of fibre with astonishing facility.

Of the Virtues of Wine.

Of all the liquors which the ingenuity of man has drawn from the productions of nature, wine may be said to be, at the same time, the most varied in its nature, the most excellent in its quality, and the most extended in its use.

Besides its tonic and strengthening power, it is more or less nutritious and salutary in every respect. The faculty of fortifying the understanding, was attributed to it by the ancients, Plato, Æschylus, and Solomon, being agreed in according to it, this virtue. But no writer has treated better of the properties of wine, than the celebrated Galen, who has assigned to each kind its proper uses, and described the differences effected in it by age, climate, &c.

Excess in the use of wine, has in all ages excited the censure of legislators. It was customary with the Greeks, to prevent the effects of this excess, by rubbing the temples and forehead with tonic ointment. Every one knows the famous trait of the legislator, who, to restrain the intemperance of the people, authorized it by an express law; and Lycurgus, as is well known, exposed a drunken slave in the streets, to impress the youth of Lacedemon, with a horror for the vice of intoxication. A law of Carthage, prohibited the use of wine during war; Plato interdicted it to young people below 22 years of age, and Aristotle to nurses and children.

In spite, however, of the wisdom of laws, and in spite of the hideous pictures presented by intemperance, the attraction of wine becomes so powerful for some men, as to degenerate into a passion. We daily see men, in other respects estimable and wise, contracting, by degrees, the habit of immoderate indulgence in this beverage, till they drown, in wine, their intellectual faculties, and their physical powers—

"Narratur et prisci Catonis
"Sæpe mero incaluisse virtus."

The qualities of wine differ according to its age; new wine is flatulent, indigestible, and purgative. They are only light wines which can be drunk before they are old.

New wines, in consequence of the quantity of carbonic acid they contain, easily induce drunkenness. The acid, disengaging itself by the heat of the stomach, quenches the irritability of the organs, and produces stupor. This theory is founded on the experiments of Bergmann, who has ascertained, that carbonic acid produces its mortal effects, by extinguishing all irritability, to such an extent, that the heart of persons who have been suffocated by this gas, exhibit no sign of it. It is known, also, that a limb, exposed for some time to the atmosphere of carbonic acid gas, becomes numb. It is not, then, to be wondered at, that, when a large quantity of it disengages in the stomach, from liquor swallowed in too great abundance, there should result torpidity, stupor, and intoxication.

Old wines are in general tonic, and very wholesome, suitable for debilitated stomachs, and for old people, and in all cases where it is desirable to give strength. They afford little nourishment, because they have been divested of their strictly nutritive principles, and contain scarcely any other principle than alcohol. It is wine of this nature that the poet speaks of, when he says,

"—————— generosum et lene requrio
" Quod curas abigat, quod cum spe divite manet,
" In venas animumque mecum, quod verba ministret,
" Quod me, Lucane, juvenem commended amicæ."

Rich luscious wines are the most nutritious; watery wines, and those which contain little sugar, are so in a very trifling degree.

Wines also differ essentially with regard to their colour; red wines are in general more spirituous, more light, and more digestible; white wines furnish less alcohol, are more diuretic, and weaker; as they have fermented less, they are almost always more rich, more nutritive, and more gareous than the red.

Pliny admits four colours of wine, white, yellow, blood-coloured, and black. It would be as minute as useless, to multiply shades which might become infinite.

Climate, culture, and differences in the management of fermentation, are also causes of infinite diversity in the qualities and virtues of wines, as has already been explained.

It appears that the ancients practised the custom of tempering their wines by an admixture of water. Pliny speaks of a wine, which, according to Homer, supported 20 parts of water; and the same naturalist informs us, that in his own times, they had wines so spirituous, that they could not be drunk, *nisi pervincerentur aqua.*

The distillation of wines has given a new value to this production of the earth: not only has it furnished a new drink, more strong and more incorruptible, but it has supplied to the arts a genuine dissolvent of resins, and, at the same time, a simple and certain means of preserving all animal and vegetable substances from decomposition.

It is in these remarkable properties that the arts of the varnisher, the perfumer, and the *liquorist* have been successively established, besides others which are founded on the same basis.

CHAPTER EIGHTH.

Of the Principles contained in Wine.

WE have already followed out the analysis of wine in the cask, in observing it gradually precipitate tartar, lees, and colouring principle, leaving little else to examine, than the alcohol, which may be extracted by fire. But this spontaneous analysis, which shews us, separately, the principles of wine, enlightens us little as to their nature; and it is necessary, by a more exact method, to supply the deficiency.

We distinguish, in all wines, an acid, alcohol, tartar, extractive matter, aroma, and a colouring principle; the whole diluted, or dissolved, in a greater or less proportion of water.

The Acid of Wine.

Malic acid exists in all wines, none having been found which do not indicate its presence in some degree. The sweetest and most luscious wines, redden blue paper, if they are allowed to remain a little time upon it; but all are not acid in the same degree. There are wines, of which the principal character is a natural acidity; those which are the produce of unripened grapes, or such as have grown on wet soils, are those of this description, while those which result from the fermentation of very rich and sugary grapes, afford very little acid. The acid thus seems to be in inverse proportion to the saccharine principle, and to the alcohol resulting from the decomposition of the sugar.

This acid exists abundantly in verjuice, and is found in must, though in very small proportion. All fermented liquors, such as cider, perry, beer, as well as fermented farinaceous matters, contain it; and Chaptal has also detected it in molasses. It is even completely to saturate it, that lime, ashes, and other earthy or alkaline bases, are employed in the purification of sugars;—were it not removed, it would prevent the crystallization of the sugar.

The malic acid disappears in the acetification of wine; in well made vinegar, there exists only the acetic acid.

The existence, in different proportions, of malic acid in wine, explains a phenomenon of the highest importance relative to the distillation of wines, and the nature of the spirits resulting from them. It is well known, that not only all wines do not yield the same quantity of spirits, but that the spirits are not nearly of the same quality. It is generally known, also, that beer, cider, perry, and fermented grains, yield little spirit, and always of a bad quality; careful and repeated distillations, it is true, may correct their defects, in a certain degree, but never entirely remove them. These constant results of long experience, have been referred to the greater quantity of extractive matter contained in these weakly vinous liquors; the combustion of a part of this extractive matter, has been considered as an immediate effect of distillation, and the acrid and empyreumatic taste, a natural result. But Chaptal having examined the subject more closely, perceived, that, besides the causes depending upon the extractive principle, it was necessary, in almost all cases, to recognize another, viz. the presence of malic acid; in fact, having distilled, with much care, these different spirituous liquors, he constantly obtained an acidulated spirit, whose taste was altered by the essential character of malic acid. It was only by restricting the distillation to the most volatile of the liquors, that a small quantity of alcohol, free from alteration, was separated, and it still preserved a disagreeable odour, from which pure spirit is free.

Wines which contain the most malic acid, yield the worst spirit. It even appears, that the quantity of alcohol is small, in proportion as the malic acid is abundant. If by means of lime-water, chalk, or a fixed alkali, this acid is removed, still a very small quantity of alcohol is obtained by distillation, and the quality is not ameliorated, for in all these cases it takes a disagreeable taste.

Tartar.

Tartar exists in the juice of the unripe grape; it is also found in the must, and, as has already been observed, concurs to the formation of alcohol, by facilitating fermentation.

When the vine is in a state of rest, it is deposited on the interior of the cask, and forms a crust, more or less thick, of imperfectly formed crystals.

When, sometime before the vintage, the casks are prepared for the reception of the new wine, the tartar is detached from them, and reserved for the demands of commerce.

Tartar is not afforded by all wines in the same proportion; red wines yield more than white, the highest coloured and most gross generally furnishing the most; there is a great difference also in the colour, and it receives the name of white or red tartar, according as it is produced from red or white wine.

This salt is very slightly soluble in cold water; it is much more so in boiling water; it scarcely dissolves in the mouth, and resists the pressure of the tooth.

It is freed from its colouring principle, by a very simple process, and afterwards bears the name of cream of tartar. With this view, it is dissolved in boiling water, and, when the water is fully saturated, it is exposed in earthen pans to cool. While cooling, it precipitates a stratum of crystals, which are already almost free from colour; these crystals are dissolved anew in boiling water, four or five per cent. of an argillaceous and sandy earth being added, and it is again evaporated. The crystals which are now precipitated, are exposed on cloths in the open air, and, after a few days exposure, they acquire that whiteness which belongs to cream of tartar: the mother waters are reserved to renew the process. Such is about the method practised at Montpellier and its environs, where almost all the manufactories of cream of tartar are established.

The vegeto-animal, or extractive principle, is abundant in the must; when fermentation changes the saccharine matter, it is sensibly diminished. A portion, almost reduced to the state of fibre, is then precipitated; it is principally this which constitutes the lees, and it is always mingled with a considerable quantity of tartar which it envelops.

There exists always in wine, a portion of vegeto-animal principle in exact dissolution, which may be obtained by the evaporation of the liquid. It is more abundant in new than in old wines. It is this lees of which wines are divested, by racking off. It is only a slight alteration of the vegeto-animal principle, or *vegetable albumen* of Leguin.

Aroma, or Bouquet.

All natural wines have a perfume, more or less agreeable. Some of them, Burgundy wines, for example, owe the greatest part of their reputation to the odour they exhale; this perfume is strengthened by age, it is rarely found in very strong wines, either because it is masked by the odour of the alcohol, or because it has been dissipated during the lengthened fermentation such wines require.

This perfume is not capable of being extracted to add to other substances; the fire seems even to destroy it, for, with the exception of a little of the liquid which first passes over in distillation, and which, in a slight degree, preserves the peculiar odour of the wine, the spirit contains no other character than those which essentially belong to it.

Colouring Principle.

The colouring principle of the wine, exists in the skin of the grape. When the wine is fermented without the marc, the wine is white. The colouring principle is not dissolved in the liquor till the alcohol is developed; it is not till then that the wine colours, and the colour is strengthened, in proportion to the length of time the wine has remained in the vat. When, however, the grapes are carefully trod, enough of colouring matter is generally mixed with the must, to give a sufficiently dark colour to the wine; and, when a wine quite discoloured is wanted, the grapes are gathered, covered with dew, and pressed as little as possible.

The colouring principle is partly precipitated in the cask, with the tartar and lees; and, when the wine is old, it is not uncommon to see it quite discoloured. The colour is then deposited in scales, on the sides and bottom of the vessel, and is seen in membranes floating in the liquor. If wine is exposed in bottles, for a few days to the sun, the colouring principle is precipitated in large flakes, without the wine losing its perfume or its strength.

The coloured precipitate is insoluble in cold or hot water, these liquids do not even produce any change in the colour. Alcohol has scarcely any effect, causing it only to take a slight brown tinge. It is dissolved by nitric acid.

When wine is reduced to the state of extract, alcohol, added to it, is coloured strongly, and water is also coloured, though in a less degree. But, besides the colouring principle which is then dissolved, there is a saccharine extractive principle which facilitates the dissolution.

The colouring principle, does not then appear of the nature of resins.; it presents all the characters belonging to a very numerous class of vegetable products, which are analogous to fecula, without possessing all its properties. The greatest number of colouring principles are of this description; they are soluble with the aid of extractive matter, but, when separated from it, they are strongly fixed.

Alcohol.

Alcohol is a transparent colourless fluid; its specific gravity, when well freed from water, is, according to Richter and Guy Lussac, 0·792, at a temperature of 68° of Fahrenheit.

Its odour is penetrating, and its taste pungent. In close vessels, it boils at a temperature of 165°. The density of its vapour is, according to Guy Lussac, 1·613.

It does not freeze at a degree of cold, equal to 122° of Fahrenheit.

Alcohol is extracted from all vinous liquors by distillation.

The existence of alcohol in vinous liquors was generally admitted, till Fabroni endeavoured to prove, that it owed its formation to the action of the fire in distillation. The facts, however, which Guy Lussac has opposed to the doctrine of the Tuscan chemist, are so conclusive, that the existence of alcohol in wine, seems now beyond a doubt, as the following, among many other experiments, prove :—

If very finely pounded, litharge is added to wine, till it becomes limpid as water, and it is then saturated with subcarbonate of potash, the alcohol separates, and collects on the surface.

If wine is distilled in vacuo, at a temperature of 50°, a very alcoholic product is obtained.

All vinous liquors which yield alcohol, do not yield it in the same proportion. Mr. Baude, who has compared the products which he obtained from the distillation of sixty-one kinds of vinous liquors, has ascertained, that they yield from 25·41 to 1·28.

CHAPTER NINTH.

Of the Manufacture of Vinegar from Wine.

IN a former chapter of this work, the acid degeneration of wine was treated of as a malady, which it was desirable to prevent or correct, though in wine countries, it generally happens, that, in spite of their efforts to the contrary, more vinegar is produced than is requisite for their wants. As it is sometimes an object with the possessor of wine to convert it into vinegar, it may be advantageous to give a short account of the most approved methods of making vinegar from wine.

Acetic acid, or vinegar, is the product of the acetous fermentation, which always follows the vinous fermentation, when the liquor is kept under circumstances favourable for it. By any one who has read the preceding parts of this treatise, these may be well ascertained from the precautions recommended to guard against it. They are, principally, the existence of a portion of leaven, the free contact of the air, and a certain degree of heat.

Vinegar may be produced from any substance which has undergone the vinous fermentation, such as cider, perry, beer, &c. and from many vegetable substances which are incapable of it; but that which is made from wine, is the purest, strongest, and best flavoured. The strength of the vinegar is also in proportion to the quantity of alcohol contained in the wine. The most ancient process for obtaining vinegar, is that described by Boerhave; it consists, in placing under a temperature of from 72° to 80° of Fahrenheit, two tubs or casks, having a grating fixed within a few inches of their bottom. On this grating is placed a close layer of green vine branches, and the casks are then filled with grape stalks. Wine is now poured in, till one of the casks is full, and the other half full; after twenty-four hours, the half filled cask is filled from the other; and, after twenty-four hours more, the other is filled from it. This process is daily repeated, till the vinegar is made. By this method of assisting fermentation, it should be completed in 15 or 20 days.

The green branches are necessary to supply the vegeto-animal principle, of which the wine may have been entirely freed, and, without which, it would lose its colour, and become bitter, but would not pass to acid. It would appear, however, from the proceeds about to be described, that it is of great importance to the excellence and flavour of the vinegar, that it should be made from wine well clarified, and consequently freed from this principle; and acetic acid, already formed, is, therefore, used to supply its place in causing fermentation.

In the city of Orleans, extensive establishments have been formed for the manufacture of vinegar, and their produce supplies almost all the north of France, and enjoys a very high celebrity. The processes there used, may, therefore, be regarded as the best, and they may be reduced to the following:—

The wine about to be converted into vinegar, is finely clarified, by being some time kept in casks, on a layer of beech chips, which separates and retains its fine lees.

The mother casks, as those in which the vinegar is made are called, are generally of sufficient capacity, to contain 400 Paris pints, (nearly 100 gallons) and, when an establishment is to be formed, those which have been previously so employed are preferred; if it is impossible to procure these, the new ones are saturated with vinegar.

They are ranged in three rows, one above another, having an aperture in the upper part, of two inches diameter, which is always kept open.

The operation is commenced, by pouring into each cask, 100 pints of boiling vinegar, of a good quality, which is suffered to remain eight days, till the casks are full; but this quantity is increased or diminished, and the additions made, at shorter or longer intervals, according to the strength of fermentation. This is judged of, by thrusting a stick into the aperture, on withdrawing which, a white scum is observed at the line of immersion, and the larger or smaller proportion of this scum, indicates a stronger or weaker fermentation.

Fifteen days after the casks are filled, the vinegar is drawn off for sale, but the casks are never more than half emptied, when wine is again added as before. The heat of the cellar in summer, is generally sufficiently high; but in winter, recourse is had to stoves, by which it is always kept at a temperature above 65° of Fahrenheit.

In most households in the country, a simple and effectual plan is resorted to for having a constant supply of good vinegar. A cask of good vinegar is purchased to commence with; it is placed near the kitchen fire, and is not firmly closed; when any quantity of its contents is drawn off for the use of the family, an equal quantity of wine (sour if they have it) is added. The colour of the vinegar is always the same as that of the wine from which it has been made, but fainter.

In all wine countries, vinegars are also made from the stalks and husks of the grapes, from the residue of distillation, &c.

If the stalks are carefully dried in the sun, and afterwards impregnated with a generous wine, the acid fermentation is established.

The husks of the grapes, after the juice has been expressed, heat by the contact of the air, and all the liquid with which they are impregnated, passes to acid.

The vinegar produced from the residue of distillation, is of a very weak description.

Vinegar always retains a portion of extractive matter, of which it is necessary to divest it. To render it pure, distillation is the readiest method; but, besides being a costly process, it deprives the vinegar of its perfume, and gives it an empyreumatic odour. The following means are sufficient to clarify it: pouring a glass of boiling milk into each cask; and, after agitating it, allowing it to settle; when a deposit is formed, the colour becomes pale, and the aroma is preserved.

CHAPTER TENTH.

Of the Distillation of Wines.

THE discovery of the art of procuring the spirituous principle of wine by distillation, has made known a new product, which is not only employed as a drink, but as a substance which has concurred most powerfully to the advancement of the arts. The product of the distillation of wines is known in commerce, under the appellation of brandy, spirit of wine, &c. but, in the language of chemistry, both these substances, which only differ in their degree of concentration, are known by the generic name, *alcohol*.

The discovery of the art of distillation has given a new importance to the productions of the vineyard. It is not now confined to the production of an agreeable drink, but a volatile, spirituous, and inflammable principle, being disengaged from it, a beverage is obtained, more active than the first, and the use of which, has become most generally extended; while, by the arts, it has been made available to dissolve resins, to form varnishes, to preserve fruits, to dissolve the perfume of plants, and, in fine, new arts have been established by its aid.

At the present day, a large proportion of the white wines, and many of the red wines, of middling quality, are submitted to distillation.

It does not appear that the ancients had any distinct idea of what is now understood by the word distillation, though Dioscorides informs us, that in distilling pitch, the volatile parts must be received in cloths; and the first navigators of the Grecian Archipelago, obtained fresh water, by holding sponges above the vessels, in which the water of the ocean was made to boil. Pliny, who, in the first century of the Christian era, treated of the vine and wine under every point of view, makes no mention of its distillation; and Galen, who wrote a century later, is equally silent on the subject.

There is every reason to believe, that the art of distillation took its rise in Arabia, and it appears that the word *alembick*, so intimately conjoined with it, can be traced to the Arabic language. It seems to have been sufficiently known to them as early as the tenth century; for Avicenne, a writer of that period, compares a catarrh to a distillation, of which the stomach is the still, the head, the head and the nose the spout through which the humours run.

Raymond Lulle, who lived in the thirteenth century, says, that the spirit was sometimes seven times rectified, but that three times were sufficient to obtain alcohol, which would burn without leaving a watery residue. He speaks much of the virtues of a preparation of brandy, called *quinta essentia;* (whence the word quintessence) and by him and his successors, this was made the base of their alchymic researches.

From this time, till the commencement of the eighteenth century, various improvements were proposed for the improvement of the apparatus used in distillation; and, in the writings of some very early authors on the subject, may be traced the germ of improvements, which it required the present state of chemical science to bring to perfection.

The happy idea, of obtaining at one boiling, a spirit of different degrees of concentration, and of carrying it at once, to that degree which commonly required repeated distillations, may be found in a treatise *de distillationibus*, by Jean Baptiste Porta, a Neapolitan, who lived towards the end of the sixteenth century, and in the writings of Dr. Arnaud, of Lyons, in 1665; and the idea is still carried farther, in the work of Jean Rodolphe Glauber, published at Amsterdam, in 1658.

During the eighteenth century, much was written on the subject of distillation, but it was bounded to the improvement of the boilers and apparatus, and the happy idea of the ancients being lost sight of, the art was almost retrograde during a century.

Towards the end of the eighteenth century, when science began to view the operations of art with a more attentive and judicious eye, the attention of Chaptal was drawn to the subject of distillation, and the improvements which he suggested, and those which have been founded upon them, gave a new aspect to the art. The attention of the brothers Argand, being about the same time engaged in the improvement of furnaces, another important alteration arose from this; and, at the present day, the labours of these philosophers, and of others who successively improved upon their suggestions, or added their own, have carried the art of distillation, in France, to a degree of perfection which would almost seem to place it beyond the want, or the reach, of further improvement.

Before this period, the apparatus most generally employed for distillation, consisted of three parts, viz. a round boiler or still, containing about 100 gallons, straitened towards the top, where it was fixed to the head, which communicated by a lengthened pipe, with a serpentine pipe or worm. The worm was placed in a cask, in which a constant supply of cold water was kept to condense the vapour.

This gross apparatus presented many deficiencies. In the first place, all the vapour which was raised by the action of the fire, passed into the worm, so that when condensed there, it contained a very large proportion of water, in consequence of the aqueous vapour which was mixed with the alcoholic, and it was found necessary to re-distil the very weak wine produced. Another defect of this apparatus was, that the worm not being sufficiently long, and the cask in which it was plunged, not sufficiently capacious, a large portion of the alcoholic vapour passed uncondensed, and mingling with the air of the cellar, occasioned a certain loss. A third defect inherent in this apparatus, was the following:—As all the vapour raised from the still, passed immediately to the worm, it was necessary to moderate the fire, in such a manner, as to allow as little as possible, of aqueous vapour to pass. Too sudden, and too strong a fire, would raise an immense portion of the water into vapour, and the spirit resulting, would, of course, be very weak; it was, consequently, necessary to watch the fire with extreme care, and the operation became difficult to conduct, and its product very expensive.

These defects, united in the distilling apparatus, made it impossible to extract the last portions of alcohol contained in the wine, without their being charged with an immense portion of water; and it was thus necessary to separate this last product of distillation, and to re-distil it with the new wine.

The spirit obtained by this process, had constantly a burnt taste, and was rarely very limpid; all which was owing to the difficulty of managing the fire, and the still greater difficulty, of obtaining all the spirit without forcing the heat.

If to this be added, that the furnace of these alembicks was ill constructed, that it afforded no means of regulating the heat, or of applying it equally over the body of the liquid, it will readily be perceived, that the art of distillation was still in its infancy.

Chaptal saw these defects, and essayed to correct them. He caused a still to be constructed of less depth, and greater width, to present a greater surface, and less depth of the liquor to the heat; he surrounded the head with a bath of cold water, to condense and separate a portion of the aqueous vapour, and make it fall back in drops, or small currents, to the still; he multiplied the circumvolutions of the worm, and enlarged the tun in which it was placed, that the water might be less easily heated; and, when to these alterations were added, the improvements of M. M. Argand on the furnace, which had brought it to an admirable degree of perfection, the ameliorations were considerable, and, during fifteen or twenty years, were applied with great success. But, during the first years of the present century, the art began to be established on new principles; and, of late, has left far behind all that was previously known or practised.

A chemical apparatus*, by means of which, vapour or gas was made to saturate liquids, by passing through them, suggested to Edward Adam, the first idea of his distilling apparatus.

The knowledge of the fact, that aqueous vapours are condensed, at a degree of heat which will not cause the condensation of alcoholic vapours, furnished him the means of completing it. Setting out from these fundamental principles, he constructed apparatus, which seemed to have remedied every thing deficient in the former practice. He obtained a patent for his inventions, and immediately, immense establishments were commenced by him, in various parts of France. But, so true is it, that the greatest improvements are only gradually, and by the spur of necessity, introduced, that, not long after, other distillers, who found it impossible to compete with Adam, sought, by im-

---

* Woulf's apparatus.

proving his apparatus, or varying it, to place themselves on a level with him. Accordingly, Isaac Berard, of Grand Gallargues, produced an apparatus, which, from its simplicity, was universally preferred to that of Adam. M. Adam attacked its inventor as having infringed his patent, and the expensive processes he was obliged to sustain against Berard and many others, overthrew his establishments; and this man, to whom we almost owe the art of distillation, died of chagrin, and in a state bordering on misery.

About the same time, M. Cellier, of Blumenthal, conceived the happy idea of multiplying almost *ad infinitum*, the surfaces of wine submitted to distillation, to save time and fuel[*]. In consequence, he

---

[*] On reading this passage, the extent to which the principle of economizing time was carried, by the ingenuity of the Scotch distillers, will probably occur to the recollection of the reader. "At the commencement of the License Act, in 1786, the duty "was thirty shillings per gallon on the capacity of the stills; "and the large stills which were then employed, were worked "off five or six times in twenty-four hours. Two years after- "wards, the duty was doubled; and the improved stills were run "off twenty times in twenty-four hours. The duty was still "further increased, till, in 1797, it was raised to the enormous "sum of £54 per gallon. Every expedient that ingenuity "could devise, was then applied to accelerate the process, and "by enlarging the width, and diminishing the depth of the still, "it could be run off seventy-two times in twenty-four hours;

made the current of vapours, which escape from the cauldron, to pass under numerous plates, placed one above another, and each containing a stratum of wine, of about an inch in thickness; these plates were constantly supplied with hot wine from the worm, and their overplus carried back to the boiler.

This process, though protected by a patent, was also imitated, and M. Cellier has shared the lot of Adam, by the process he instituted against those who had infringed his patent; so inefficient are the laws relative to patents in France.

Since that time, many improvements, originating in the same principles, have been introduced; and, by the apparatus now employed in the best French distilleries, it is possible to obtain at once a spirit at any, or at all degrees of concentration, from a weak brandy, to the purest alcohol, free from empyreuma; and, while there is the greatest saving of fuel and manual labour, a much greater proportion of spirit is obtained from the same wine, than

---

" and at last, the improvements reached so high a degree of perfection, that the time between charge and charge, was not more than three minutes, and even this was exceeded in another experiment, where a still was run off nearly twenty-two times in the hour." "Millar's Chemistry, applied to the Phenomena of Nature and the Processes of the Arts."—W. & C. Tait, Edinburgh, 1820.

formerly. The improvements are applicable, in a peculiar degree, to the distillation of fermented grain, beer, the husks of the grape, &c. as a more perfect spirit is obtained, free from the burnt taste, or empyreuma, and the cauldron is not burned, as it is wont to be, when husks or grains are distilled on the naked fire. In no case is it necessary to re-distil the spirit obtained.

All wines, and all fermented liquors generally, do not furnish the same quantity of spirit, nor spirit of the same quality; the wines of a warm climate yield more than those of a colder climate. In the south of France, a third is sometimes obtained, and the average is a fourth; while, in the central districts, it is only a fifth, and in the north, from a sixth to a tenth.

A great difference is sometimes observed in the spirituosity of the wines of vineyards in the same district: vines exposed to the south, and planted in a light and dry soil, generally produce wines strongly charged with alcohol; while those close beside them, if under a different exposure, and on a strong and damp soil, yield wines extremely weak, and destitute of spirit.

The strength of wines may be deduced from the portion of alcohol they yield, but their goodness, their quality, their price in commerce, cannot be estimated on this basis. The bouquet, or perfume, and the taste, which make them most in request, are qualities distinct from, and independent of, the quantity of alcohol they contain.

Generally speaking, wines rich in alcohol are strong and generous, but they have neither the delicacy nor the perfume which characterize some others; the spirit resulting from these, is less agreeable than that from weaker wines.

White wines, yield a better tasted brandy than red wines. Almost throughout the south of France, they distil red wines; but the brandy, although more abundant, is less esteemed than that of the white wines distilled in the east.

Wines which have commenced changing to acidity, afford little spirit, and it is of a bad quality; this is owing to the alcohol having, by the commencement of acetification, undergone a degree of decomposition which alters its virtues, and its having formed an acid which rises mixed with the alcohol.

It is only, then, well fermented, and well kept wines, which ought to be distilled; and this accounts for the opinion of all distillers, that it is most advantageous to distil wines the moment they have terminated their fermentation. It is well to observe, however, that this principle is only applicable to inferior wines, which are easily changed; for strong, well fermented, and well clarified wines, may be distilled at any time.

Before the wine is committed to it, the boiler or

still, is washed with the greatest care; and, in the case where a distillation is just terminated, the cock is opened to give issue to the waste (*vinasse*), and a baton introduced, to detach every thing which may adhere to the bottom of the boiler; after which, water is poured in, and, after being allowed to remain some time, is run off.

To understand all the importance of this preliminary operation, it need only be observed, that if such precautions are neglected, the interior of the boiler is soon covered with a crust of tartar and lees, which gives a bad taste to the spirit, and causes the calcination of the copper, which is then not immediately wetted by the liquor.

The first spirit which passes in distillation, has neither an agreeable taste nor smell; it is separated to be re-distilled. The spirit which succeeds, is very much concentrated, and of a good quality; its strength is determined by the hydrometer, and this instrument is now placed at the opening of the receiver, to judge of the strength of the alcohol during the whole time of the operation; towards the end of which, a candle is applied to the small cock, and this is repeated, till the vapour ceases to inflame, and from that moment the operation is terminated.

The alcohol extracted by distillation, ought to be colourless, and free from bad smell. Any bad qualities it may possess, may be got rid of by re-distilling it carefully; it is even often sufficient, to filter it through charcoal, well burned, and reduced to a very fine powder. Almost always, the bad qualities of the spirit are owing to the distillation having been ill-conducted, or to the want of cleanness in the apparatus employed. It sometimes, however, happens, that its defects are owing to the wine, especially if it had commenced turning sour.

By being kept in new wood, the alcohol contracts a yellowish colour, which does not affect its quality, and in growing old, it loses that taste of fire which it frequently has when new, and becomes milder and more agreeable to the taste.

The instruments used in commerce, for ascertaining the strength of spirits, are not of a mathematical precision, but they are sufficient to give it by approximation. Before arriving at the knowledge of these instruments, many very inexact methods were used.

A regulation of France, in 1729, prescribed, that a quantity of gunpowder should be put into a spoon, and that this powder should be covered with spirit; its strength was judged of, by observing whether or not the powder inflamed when the spirit was burned; but, to have obtained an exact result, it would have been necessary that the quantity of spirit, and the quantity of powder, should have been always the same; for a greater quantity of the spirituous liquor, by leaving a larger portion of water, would prevent the combustion of the powder.

The carbonate of potash, as dissolving itself with greater or less facility, as the alcohol was more or less charged with water, was also employed.

In 1770, the Spanish government prescribed the use of oil as a liquor of proof. The process consisted in letting fall a drop of oil into the spirit, and they pronounced on the degree of spirituosity, by the depth to which the oil descended in the liquor; but it is evident, that the immersion would be proportioned to the size of the drop, and the height of the fall.

The instrument in use, in the south of France, is the very correct spirit-gage of M. M. Borie, and Pouget of Cette, invented in 1772. These able philosophers, after a course of very exact experiments on alcohol, at all degrees of concentration, and every degree of temperature, adapted the thermometer to the spirit gage, in such a manner, that the instrument itself indicates the correction necessary by the influence of temperature.

Spirits which mark from 21° to 22° of this instrument, are said to be at *Holland proof*. This first quality, more concentrated, and reduced to three-fifths, by the substraction of two-fifths of the water it contains, takes the name of *three-fifths*. It is carried to *three-sixths*, or *three-sevenths*, by divesting it of a fifth, or a fourth more of its aqueous principle.

In Paris, and elsewhere, the spirit-gage of Gartier, or Baumè, is made use of; they are less exact than that of Borie, but sufficiently so for the purposes of trade.

Alcohol is employed as a beverage; it is a dissolvent of resins, and constitutes the basis of drying varnishes.

Alcohol serves as a vehicle for the aromatic principle of plants, and takes the name of *spirit* of the plant, with the aroma of which it is impregnated. When employed by the apothecary to dissolve resins, the dissolutions formed by it receive the appellation of tinctures.

Alcohol forms the base of almost all the beverages called *liqueurs*; it is sweetened with sugar, and aromatized with all substances which have an agreeable taste or smell; prevents the fermentation and putrefaction of animal and vegetable substances, and is therefore employed in the preservation of fruits, vegetables, and animal matters.

All vegetables which have undergone the vinous fermentation, yield alcohol by distillation; but in quantity and quality exceedingly variable.

The alcohol of cider is generally ill-tasted, because this fermented liquor contains much malic acid, which rises with, and remains in the spirit.

Alcohol extracted from wild cherries, fermented, has more strength, at the same degree, than that of

74
4
——
88
✓

20/4;74
1/-

p/
o/n 2/900.

cat-4

6/-

CPSIA information can be obtained
at www.ICGtesting.com
Printed in the USA
LVHW082118121218
600229LV00012B/313/P